Museums and Racism

Racism is a hot topic in museums today, as well as an urgent social issue. Focused on the broad field of multicultural policy, *Museums and Racism* examines how the Immigration Museum in Melbourne, Australia, has responded to political culture and public debate around racism.

Analysis focuses on the conceptualization of the Immigration Museum in the mid-1990s, and on the most recent permanent exhibition to be opened there, in 2011, which coincided with the publication of a new multicultural policy for Australia. The opening of the National Museum of Australia in Canberra in the intervening period is also examined in some detail, as a comparative case study to provide a sense of the broader national social and political context. Message argues that each of the three episodes demonstrates the close relationship between museum and exhibition development on the one hand, and policy, politics, and public opinion on the other hand.

Including a discussion of examples from the United States and other relevant contexts, *Museums and Racism* is key reading for students and scholars of museum studies and cultural studies around the world. The book should also be of great interest to museum practitioners and policymakers in the area of multiculturalism.

Kylie Message is Associate Professor and Senior Fellow in the Humanities Research Centre at the Australian National University. She is the Series Editor of 'Museums in Focus'.

Museums in Focus
Series Editor: Kylie Message

Committed to the articulation of big, even risky, ideas in small format publications, 'Museums in Focus' challenges authors and readers to experiment with, innovate, and press museums and the intellectual frameworks through which we view these. It offers a platform for approaches that radically rethink the relationships between cultural and intellectual crisis and debates about museums, politics, and the broader public sphere.

'Museums in Focus' is motivated by the intellectual hypothesis that museums are not innately 'useful', safe' or even 'public' places, and that recalibrating our thinking about them might benefit from adopting a more radical and oppositional form of logic and approach. Examining this problem requires a level of comfort with (or at least tolerance of) the ideas of dissent, protest, and radical thinking, and authors might benefit from considering how cultural and intellectual crisis, regeneration and anxiety have been dealt with in other disciplines and contexts.

Recently published titles:

The Disobedient Museum
Writing at the Edge
Kylie Message

Museums and Racism
Kylie Message

https://www.routledge.com/Museums-in-Focus/book-series/MIF

⌐MUSEUMS IN FOCUS⌐

Logo by James Verdon (2017)

Museums and Racism

Kylie Message

Routledge
Taylor & Francis Group

LONDON AND NEW YORK

First published 2018 by Routledge

2 Park Square, Milton Park, Abingdon, Oxon OX14 4RN
605 Third Avenue, New York, NY 10017

Routledge is an imprint of the Taylor & Francis Group, an informa business

First issued in paperback 2021

British Library Cataloguing-in-Publication Data
A catalogue record for this book is available from the British Library

Library of Congress Cataloging-in-Publication Data
A catalog record has been requested for this book

ISBN: 978-1-138-24017-9 (hbk)
ISBN: 978-0-367-49143-7 (pbk)

Typeset in Times New Roman
by Apex CoVantage, LLC

Anonymous graffiti, Athens. Image and logo by James Verdon (2017).

For Ezra

Contents

List of illustrations

Acknowledgements

Writing this book catapulted me back to my roots. I was a curatorial assistant at the Museum of Victoria for a period in the late 1990s, where I learnt vast amounts about working across theory, case study research, and practical day-to-day museum work from inspiring, energetic, and generous museum staff including MaryAnne McCubbin, Eddie Butler-Bowden, John Kean, and Dean Wilson. I am grateful for this experience, which seeded my fascination for institutional ethnography and my understanding of museums as multifaceted conglomerations – infrastructure – that combine institutional governance and operational features largely invisible to the public with public outcomes such as exhibitions and programs. I was not involved in the Immigration Museum development, but I recall many meetings at which it was the subject of discussion for the Australian Society program area in which I was located. This book has directly benefitted from that experience, as well as from the conversations and researches that have filled the twenty years since, specifically across the institutions of Museum Victoria, the National Museum of Australia, the University of Melbourne, and the Australian National University, and with individuals to whom I owe a special debt of thanks for formative conversations about museums, politics, diversity, mobilities, and migration: Howard Morphy, Mary Hutchison, Paul Pickering, Jakob Parby, and Laurence Gouriévidis. I warmly acknowledge Ezra Johnston for the insight and guidance he provided about sequels and trilogies.

Set against this background, much of the research that has informed this book was supported by the Australian Government through the Australian Research Council's *Discovery Projects* funding scheme (DP 120100594) for 'Collecting institutions, cultural diversity and the making of citizenship in Australia since the 1970s', a project led by Andrea Witcomb (Deakin University) that involved Ian McShane (RMIT) and myself, as well as Simon Knell (University of Leicester) and Arne Bugge Amundsen (University of Oslo), with research assistance by Philipp Schorch and Karen

Schamberger. The project drew on numerous institutional archives in Australia, with the Immigration Museum and Museum Victoria being most relevant for this particular book. Moya McFadzeon (Immigration Museum) has provided ongoing support throughout the project, and the idea for this book resulted from a forum, 'Owning Racism – Can We Talk?' that she organized to coincide with the launch of *Identity: yours, mine, ours* at the Immigration Museum in 2011. I am grateful to Museum Victoria for providing and approving the reproduction of images (Figures 0.1, 3.1, and 4.1). Chapter 2 is an expanded and updated version of 'Culture, citizenship and Australian multiculturalism: the contest over identity formation at the National Museum of Australia', *Humanities Research,* XV (2), 2009: 23–48, and I acknowledge ANU Press for permission to use this work in the very different context of this book. Additionally, I am very grateful for a period of research leave provided by the Australian National University, which enabled the completion of this book. I continue to be indebted to Heidi Lowther and the editorial team at Routledge for their continuing support and commitment to the Museums in Focus series.

Finally, although this book has relied primarily on archival research, much of the writing has occurred at kitchen tables rather than offices or desks, in various places, over several years. I am indebted to everyone who shared their stories, experiences, lives, and tables with me and mine. This includes my family – Guy Jones, Oscar Johnston and Ezra Johnston, as well as Bob and Jill Message – who have lived and contributed to this book in too many ways to mention, and to whom I am endlessly grateful.

It's a summer of sequels. The culture wars are back. So is the civil rights movement[1]

Three-way thinking

Last year I set myself the task of trying to complete three related books in close succession. I wanted to start playing out some of the questions I was asking authors contributing to the Museums in Focus series to examine. I was motivated less by a desire to privilege any particular disciplinary approach than by the intention to test out different ideas about how we think about museums and extend processes of self-reflection to the exercise of writing about them. As short books, my rationale went, they could be more responsive to contemporary events and change, more experimental and process oriented. The quick production time and electronic publication also appealed. The books would circulate in the public sphere alongside the topics and debates upon which they were commenting. My intention was to retain proximity between the books and their context in the hope that this approach would counteract some of the concerns that critique can fetishize the expert authority who operates at a distance.[2] Furthermore, although the research and scholarship had to be of the highest quality, the books could be published as critical engagements with events and actions, reflections on previous thinking about a topic, they could profile moments in time, or function as works-in-progress. The links and conversations that exist and might be created *between* the books and other forms of theorizing about museums, culture, and politics – based in museum studies or not – would, I hope, become a more significant outcome of the series than any individual book itself.

It also so happened that 2016 and 2017 were flashpoint years in terms of political and cultural action in the places I was working. The culture wars returned to the United States (Cotter 2017), as they did in Australia, where they were repackaged as the wittily named 'statue wars' (Bongiorno 2017).[3] Political and public anxiety and occurrences of racism grew in both countries, particularly over issues around immigration and asylum seekers. My

Figure 0.1 'Who's Next Door?' tram installation, *Identity: yours, mine, ours* exhibition, Immigration Museum

Photograph by Benjamin Healley. Image courtesy of Museum Victoria.

project gained urgency as I reflected on the case studies I was developing and the task I had set myself, and with dwindling confidence about any prospect that the summer would yield closure, I decided to structure my books around a trilogy model. Although my trilogy may not ultimately deliver an outcome or resolution to political strife, it might, I hope, contribute to understandings about the role of museums, culture, and critical thinking in times of political crisis.

Throughout the period of writing (which is ongoing – book three is still in progress), the trilogy model has become increasingly useful for organizing and articulating how the goals of each book link to each other and relate to the general aims I have established for the broader series. It has provided me with a framework to clearly demonstrate that each volume has a distinct purpose/case study/concern/research question/approach that relates to the other books, but that also exists independent of the others. Viewed in relation to the formula typically associated with a trilogy, the first book, *The Disobedient Museum: Writing at the Edge*, establishes 'What's wrong with the world/discipline/other contextual field' through its analysis of socio-political and disciplinary crisis and dissent. It makes a case for the research question that is being asked. The second book (this one), *Museums and Racism*, is the 'Now We Know What's Wrong With Our World, and This is What We're Going to do to Fix It book' (Johnson 2012). It has its own 'plot' and set of problems, but its purpose is to provide the defining moment for the series. Book two of a trilogy is usually where the consequences of the overreaching concern are suddenly made clear. This means that – in fiction at least – book two is 'where the main character knows exactly what they're up against, and even how far the antagonist will go to achieve their diabolical ends. . . . The main character will often experience a profound All is Lost moment'.

In my trilogy, book two is about racism. Its concern is with the structure and the apparatus and exercise of power, specifically in relation to observations that racism is increasing in many nations, including in a Donald Trump-led USA, about which anthropologist Sindre Bangstad (2017) has made the observation that hate crimes 'tend to increase when powerful figures engage in it or provide licence and legitimacy to it' (also see Posner and Neiwert 2016). The challenge faced by book two in any three-book series is to show 'what we are up against'. This book is no different, and my challenge here is to show some elements of the experience and 'management' (Shoshan 2016) of racism and hate speech as they have been represented, examined, and in some cases counteracted by museums. I determined that focusing book two – which emphasizes the depth of a given problem – on a specific (albeit partial) institutional case study was an appropriate way to extend the aims of the series whilst utilizing the opportunities and expectations for contextualization, comparison, and extension that become available within the trilogy formula.

As I researched what trilogies do and how they work, their formula (and the ways in which people read 'across' volumes within trilogies) came to gain increasing relevance for my project. This sub-set of the Museums in Focus series was designed to be tri-partite from the get-go: a series of books that would engage respectively with and examine the structures of writing (book one), the structures of governance (book two), and the structures of resistance (book three). While a desire to critically engage with the concept and experience of structure (be it institutional, socio-political, cultural, or disciplinary) underpins all three books, a key intention of this trilogy is to also acknowledge and explore different methodologies for exploring the functions and outcomes as well as the expressions of resistance against structure. While each book in the trilogy is bound to the others by a shared investigation of structure, and work, as such, to expand the theoretical engagement initiated by the previous volume, they also individually offer a different museological focus. Museums (and the museum-like activities and places that are included in my expansive use of the term, see Message 2018) are at the heart of my trilogy because they so frequently operate as sites that bring diverse and sometimes conflicting expressions of power and authority into contact (including in relation to internal operations, staffing, and structures, see Fischer, Anila and Moore 2017). So, while each book in the trilogy has been designed with a different goal and purpose, they have a common interest in investigating the role of museums as sites of both structure and resistance in the field of contemporary activism.

The trilogy is organized in the following way. Book one, *The Disobedient Museum: Writing at the Edge* takes as its case study the process of writing about museums. It gives an overview of social and disciplinary action in the field of cultural politics pertaining to museums, and it builds a theoretical rationale for the approaches taken in the two case study-focused books that follow. The main case study at the heart of book two, *Museums and Racism*, is the Immigration Museum, a government-run public museum in the Australian state of Victoria (located in the state's capital, Melbourne) – that I investigate to consider the approach taken by one institution in dealing with a contentious contemporary social issue – racism – from within a structural perspective and political context. The third book, *Curatorial Activism, Archiving Occupy*, offers the contrasting example of an 'anti-governmental' case study of a working group active within the Occupy Wall Street Movement, in the United States in 2011. Its focus is a non-institutional 'museum-like' event (what is described in book one as a 'context') that aimed to create an alternately structured and non-hierarchical field of political culture. In comparison with book two's firm focus on institutional actions within and in relation to the Immigration Museum and the National Museum of Australia, which is presented as a contextual case study, book three has an external purview. The purpose of that book is to undertake analysis of a political event (Occupy Wall Street) and the process of archiving elements of this in relation to a survey of institutional approaches, perspectives, and priorities.

A feature of the broader Museums in Focus book series is attention to crisp, politically engaged and self-aware writing and methodological excellence and innovation that challenges normative models of writing in the field of museum studies. *The Disobedient Museum: Writing at the Edge* initiated this process by demanding reflection of our scholarship practices to probe the question, 'What can writing about museums actually *do*?' Another feature of politically engaged self-reflective writing is attention to the effects of what we write. We do not conduct this activity in a vacuum, and our readers (like museum audiences) are not homogenous, even within the categories that we attribute to particular cohorts. As such, the trilogy of books that I am contributing to this series has been designed with the aim of exploring what writing for different audiences can look like. This is an exploratory exercise rather than a prescriptive one, and there are many other groups that could be targeted. Another approach would, for example, be to write one single case study 'three ways', with each iteration oriented toward the priorities of a different stakeholder group or point of view. That would highlight the way in which different experiences and perspectives are privileged, although it might compromise the active process of negotiation and multivocality that can occur through the process of writing a single book. A further option would be to simply write a series of 'companion books', which are essentially books that replicate the same idea, or to look for a set of similar or familiar findings from another, usually complimentary case study. These approaches do not continually build and challenge the theoretical and pragmatic parameters of the argument that is constructed, but apply a set of pre-determined outcomes to a set of different (but not too different) examples.

There are good reasons to target books at different readers, consistent with the commitment by contemporary museum studies to be inclusive, pluralist, and multivocal in its museum-focused researches and analyses (Chapter 1). My additional reason for taking this route, however, is because of my commitment to exploring and drawing attention to the exercise of *writing* about museums. I wanted to test the contention that '[T]he first draft is for the writer. The second draft is for the editor. The last draft is for the reader' (Ricks 2017). Whilst my first and second books are not rehearsals for a third book in which some monumental truth will be revealed (nor are they drafts!), they have been designed to demonstrate what the stages of writing can entail, and to demonstrate the point that our audience influences not just who we write for (and who we exclude or do not address) but how we go about that activity. Although Ricks' (2017) description of revising a single book across three drafts was influenced by advice that he turned into a mantra – 'Defer to the narrative'. . . 'Get out of the way and let the stories tell themselves' – I believe it is our job as writers to illustrate how 'the narrative' or story will be shaped by different structural contexts. It follows that the process of narrative writing should also be influenced by the readership a writer aims to communicate with, particularly in the case of scholarship about museums.

If we extend Ricks' analogy to my trilogy:

- 'The first draft is for the writer'. *The Disobedient Museum: Writing at the Edge* (book one) extends the boundaries of 'the writer' to include the discipline; that is the immediate cohort of people working within museum studies. This book is concerned with examining various conceptual models for understanding crisis and critique in disciplinary terms, and it draws from a tool-box and set of resources that are primarily theoretical and academic.
- 'The second draft is for the editor'. *Museums and Racism* (book two) interprets 'the editor' as being a broader field of museum studies which includes museum practitioners and people with specialist interests in the correlation between museums, social governance, and activism, and those reading for information about race hate speech and anti-racism in Australia. This book's focus on institutional cultures and processes in context of political and public debates about museums, migration, and multiculturalism has meant that I have focused research for this book on predominantly internal archives and collections, institutional documentation, collections, and exhibitions on the one hand, and public records such as official statements of political policy, decision-making, and public responses to both (published newspapers, media comments, and the like) on the other hand.
- 'The last draft is for the reader'. The general public that constitutes the 'reader' in Ricks' case is translated in *Curatorial Activism, Archiving Occupy* (book three) to mean community based stakeholders and non-governmentally affiliated activists and archive makers. This final book is also likely to be the most popular of the three because, oriented to the reaction of individual agents involved in the process of activism, it is narrative-driven in an affective and embodied way that the other two cannot be. Focused on a description of events – the *experience* of what happened, why and how, this narrative contrasts with that of the previous two books (the narrative of book one is disciplinary and focused on the techniques of writing; the narrative of book two is institutional and focused on intersections between the apparatus of political power and museums as sites of governance).

Even despite being drawn from different fields and types of evidence (book one – theoretical/conceptual; book two – institutional documentation, government policy, and media reporting; and book three – biographical and object based), the three books in the trilogy are linked by a shared commitment to understanding the relationship between social and political protest, museums, and other forms of cultural phenomena that generate as well as record, collect, document, archive, and exhibit. The books also share a commitment to reinvigorating the role of the public intellectual, including examining the role that museums can themselves play as public intellectuals (recognizing that this was partly the reason that museums became contested sites in the culture and history wars era in Australia and the United States).

In addition to highlighting different elements of government interactions with public opinion and activism, each book approaches its discrete subject or case study by modeling strategies drawn from different disciplinary frameworks. Because interdisciplinarity is fundamentally about interactions, be they collaborative, disputed, or ambivalent, across borders and between disciplines, it was important to consider a range of relevant constitutive elements. As such, I structured the trilogy by aligning each short book to a specific approach, set of intellectual parameters, and a correlating field of resources. Whilst I consider all books to be museum studies books first and foremost, the disciplinary alignments can roughly be described as cultural studies (book one, which asks how do we write about museums in context of socio-political and disciplinary crisis), public history (book two, focused on museums and public policy, examines how museums engage with, respond to, or reproduce socio-political crises such as structural racism), and anthropological (book three, which explores the collection and representation within museums of the material culture of crisis, and investigates how this contributes – or not – to the activism or cause being represented). A far too crude, short hand, representation of the focus of each is: book one – ideas; book two – institutions; book three – things. 'People' are central to all three (as is structure, as I have already noted, and a key emphasis of the series is representing how each of these terms acts upon and are influenced by the others).

My decision to loosely divide my guiding generalized methodological approach into its constituent parts was related to the goal for the trilogy to examine – through modeling – how we actually 'do' museum studies (rather than further mimicking 'what' it typically has 'looked like', see Message 2018). Of course, it is not the case that institutions and 'things' are missing from book one, just as it is not the case that ideas and institutions are absent from book three. It is similarly not the case that each book is completely restricted to particular disciplinary techniques and regimes. I employed this deconstructed approach as much to examine the shortcomings of any narrowly restrictive attempt, as I did to show the impossibility of disciplinary purity in any attempt to understand the relationships between thought, society, government, and resistance.

In the final instance, the trilogy advocates for engaged and grounded research methods for museum studies (Message 2018: 46–50, 75). However,

I have, in each of the three volumes, tried to highlight some of the component parts and field of sources that make up various tools in our methodological kit so that the second and third books can build on the argument and
field of knowledge explored by the previous one(s). This means that the first
book's aim to represent and model the practice of writing about museums
is expanded in the second book's critical examination of the role museums
play as political agents within society, which in turn provides the artillery
required for the third book's analysis of the way museums (and 'museum-
like' sites and events) collect, represent, and potentially contribute to crisis
and political change. The different foci of each book demand recognition
that what 'grounded research' is will be different in different contexts and
as per different research questions. For example, in some cases, research
will be grounded in archives or will be primarily paper or document based.
In other cases, it will focus on working with people through ethnographic
methods or interview based research. Whilst a traditional length monograph
would typically – and appropriately – combine these tools and approaches,
I have adopted the trilogy model to separate them so as to encourage critical thinking about methods, and to argue that the process of (re)combining
these tools must occur with rigorous understanding about, in dialogue with,
and out of respect for, the specific requirements of the case study or idea
that is being explored.

Notes

1 Cotter (2017).
2 Ignacio Farias (2011: 367) advocates for 'inquiry' over criticism, which, he says
   can only exist in theoretical mode, thereby running the risk of silencing heterogeneity. 'Inquiry', by comparison, 'involves a commitment to the empirical. This
   is the leading force. The conceptual languages we mobilize are certainly crucial,
   for they define what counts as empirical, and should therefore be subordinated
   to actual inquiries. . . . In this context, "follow the actors" does not simply mean
   "stick to your object of study", but rather "follow their inquiries".'
3 In Australia, the period and events of the late 1990s/early 2000s are referred to
   interchangeably as the 'history wars' and the 'culture wars'. I use whichever term
   is most relevant to the particular situation See Chapters 2 and 3, and Message
   (2006).

1 Museums

Museums and Racism examines the development of the Immigration Museum in Melbourne in context of contemporary developments in social and cultural policy fields around multiculturalism and debates about racism and hate speech in Australia.[1] It approaches this task by examining claims around whether museums can make a contribution to understandings about the motivations for and 'management' of hate (Shoshan 2016: 6), and the experience of structural racism.[2] This study is important because while museums frequently identify with the moral high ground, presenting themselves as arbiters of social justice and reasonableness, racism, like all forms of extremism, is considered to be a form of moral abjection anathema to rational thinking. Where museums aspire to be inclusive, and to collaborate with minority or marginalized groups to offer agency, the very purpose of racist hate speech is to inhibit the ability of the targets of hate speech to talk back. Hate speech aims at a basic level to 'exclude its targets from participating in broader deliberative processes' (Gelber 2011: 84).

The mismatch of language and moral parameters raises complex challenges for museums, particularly those with a remit to represent national identity. The situation is made more difficult still by an increasing acceptance of whiteness as a central defining marker of national identity in Australia and other postcolonial nations such as the United States, where these challenges have been recognized by many as escalating in recent months.[3] Claims of urgency show direct links between incidences of racially motivated violence in Charlottesville in the United States, where, writer Toni Morrison (2016) reminds us, 'the definition of "Americanness" is color' (and similar events in Australia, where vandalism against colonial statues have been attributed as outcomes of both Charlottesville and the 'Change the Date' campaign).[4] Renewed attention by the media to statements of overt racist hate evidence the continuity of a structural condition that has an extended history of moving race hate speech in and out of public realms of visibility and acceptance at various times.

Figure 1.1 Immigration Museum, Old Customs House, Melbourne
Photograph by Kylie Message.

In *The Disobedient Museum*, I argued for the effectiveness of structural forms of resistance that work within and through sets of cultural, political, and institutional conditions to disrupt, destabilize, and force change from within. I investigated ways to challenge accepted knowledge/received 'wisdom' about 'the museum' through a range of critical disciplinary frameworks. I argued that the form of resistance advocated in that book – disruption of a system from within – was more effective to the challenges explored there than a whole-scale rejection or revolution against systemic discrimination.[5] Arguments about how to engage with a crisis that perhaps has itself become a systemic condition or norm of contemporary life have also been articulated by a range of social movement theorists and writers in the wake of events occurring in the period following the inauguration of Trump, from the Women's Marches through to the Charlottesville clashes and protests. In an essay called 'Is there any point in protesting?' Nathan Heller employs Zeynep Tufekci's work to suggest that 'the movements that succeed are actually proto-institutional: highly organized; strategically flexible, due to sinewy management structures; and chummy with the sorts of people we now call élites'. 'Far from speaking truth to power', argues

Heller, 'successful protests seem to speak truth through power', meaning that they need to work within or through the systems they want to change.

In contrast, the hate speech and racism that is exemplified by Ku Klux Klan words and actions function through antagonism. Their tactics are confrontational and often terrifying, designed to create a sense of possibility for an alternative structure of perceived normality/normalization (Waldron 2014; Posner and Neiwert 2016; Shoshan 2016). Their aim is not to effect change within existing social structures, but to entirely reconstitute what are considered acceptable norms within society. To an extent, this approach has been a successful one for the 'alt-right', as suggested by the fact that in 2017, the Council of the District of Columbia activated its 'hate crimes protocol' (Milloy 2017). The policy assured residents that it would act swiftly in response to incidences which the District of Columbia Mayor Muriel E. Bowser identified as 'acts' of violence 'that put communities at risk' (quoted in Milloy 2017). Such statements have led some commentators to observe that the language of white supremacy seems to be trending back in by becoming a more ubiquitous feature of mainstream society. However, others have argued that:

> the nooses have always been there and will be for years to come. All the bravado about special noose-stopping protocols and promises to catch the vandals have just become part of a very predictable play. A noose is discovered. People are outraged. Protests are held. A culprit is seldom found. People forget. Then, repeat.
>
> (Milloy 2017)

In addition, the Council of the District of Columbia Committee on Public Safety and the Judiciary 2008 noted 'a rash of cases involving nooses' occurring in recent years – 50 were reported by the Southern Poverty Law Centre in 2007 alone. The conflicting aims and forms of expression and reaction apparent between the noose-leavers and the Council of the District of Columbia, for example, have created a gulf between hate speech advocates and the museums and other institutions (schools, universities, some media) which seek to provide education and other programs to counteract the effects of their words.

Acts of fear-mongering (such as leaving nooses in public places) are not just forms of distraction. They are exercises in testing or challenging the legitimacy of legislation and community standards around freedom of expression. In so doing, they reveal the tensions between maintaining freedom of expression and curbing racism in countries such as the United States, and including Australia. Political scientist Erik Bleich refers to this tension as 'a fundamental dilemma for liberal democracies' (quoted in

Bangstad 2017; also see Gelber and McNamara 2016).[6] The conundrum that is caused by the 'inevitable' dilemma means that there is little space for dialogue between museums, governmental organizations, and proponents of the extreme right.[7] The spate of nooses being reported as found in museum grounds in the United States over recent months suggests that even where such a space exists, it has been appropriated as a symbolic opportunity for further opportunity to promote fear. There is no shortage of academic analyses of free speech legislation or attempts to navigate the dilemma between how to maintain freedom of expression but condone hate speech, however, such work tends to emphasize the legal and governmental apparatus of regulation at the expense of the implications and effect of hate speech.

Bangstad (2017) recommends a different tack for studying acts of race hate. He suggests that an anthropological lens can bridge rather than exacerbate the distinctions existing between disciplines primarily affiliated with political science and legal studies, and more 'grounded forms of analysis' concerned with victim impact and the affect of certain events or conditions (Message 2018: 7). This approach requires the construction of a conversation between text (case study) and context (environment within which the museum, for example, operates). The context includes other instruments of governance such as the media and policy initiatives, both of which act upon and help shape the public sphere. The appeal of this approach is that it refuses to accept hate speech's project of excluding its targets from participating in broader deliberative processes. It also avoids the trap of closing down the discussion about hate speech that can be an outcome of debates about racism (which can risk leaning in the favour of speech restriction and thereby further silencing everyone involved). Bangstad's approach identifies the need to acknowledge spaces of communication with individuals targeted by hate speech. It resonates with the approaches that are increasingly preferred by museums and museum studies in that it:

- Starts with the real-life experiences of victims of hate speech in order to tell us 'exactly what hate speech sounds and feels like and what it does' (Bangstad 2017).
- Focuses on hate speech's relation to power, social status, race, and gender to 'elicit the often ignored or glossed over linkages between more mainstream discourses that feed on and onto hate speech' (Bangstad 2017).
- Maps the intersections and shared strategies that exist between forms of hate speech that target specific 'causes' (such as immigration, Islam, Black Lives Matter, or feminism) and that contribute to a broader culture of fear/normalization of hate speech.

Bangstad's project is a fundamentally simple – and political – one that works on the proposition that rehumanizing the victims of hate speech will be a powerful tool in the larger project of challenging the normalization of structural racism. Many of the anthropological tactics he advises have an established precedent of being widely employed in museums globally, including those with a thematic focus such as migration, human rights, genocide, but extending also to many of the institutions and places associated with the International Coalition of Sites of Conscience, as well as a very large number of national museums globally, including, perhaps most notably, the National Museum of African American History and Culture, which opened in Washington, DC, in 2017 and which includes significant commentary about race hate.

Adding to the body of politically driven academic scholarship represented by Bangstad is a rapidly growing genre of museums and exhibitions that have taken on the task of representing the experience of migration and multiculturalism from a range of perspectives. It is beyond the parameters and intention of this short book to provide a comprehensive overview of current museological activity relevant to this study, which spans migration policy, multicultural initiatives, and public discourse, debate, and experience. However the expansion of museums working with these subjects globally suggests that although it can sometimes seem as though there is little room for interaction between spheres, an increasing opportunity has actually opened up, perhaps as a consequence of the increasing ubiquity and 'mainstreaming' of hate speech in contemporary life.[8] In other words, the fact that nooses have been left on the grounds of museums reiterates the political function of culture and the significance of museums as sites of identity. I suspect that perhaps even more than in previous iterations of the 'culture wars' (Message 2006), this is one battle that museums today are willing and primed for.[9]

Extending the project of boundary crossing introduced in *The Disobedient Museum: Writing at the Edge* (Message 2018), this book sets out to represent the gulf between museums and racism as a site of exchange. Also extending the expectation that the second book of a trilogy will function as a kind of narrative bridge between the first and final books, I argue that the possibility for exchange arose as a result of the establishment of an exhibition on racism by the Immigration Museum in 2011. Although creation of a site for communication may sound an unlikely outcome from a debate on racism, the Immigration Museum's tools were sharpened by its alertness and responsiveness to decades of debate within the Australian state of Victoria over policy initiatives around migration, refugee and asylum seeker protocols, and public perspectives on political culture and the influence of multiculturalism and cultural diversity. This readiness was also influenced by the museum's observations of the contestation surrounding the National Museum of Australia, which was involved in a very public debate about race and identity from 2001 to 2003. Indeed, the relationship between the Immigration Museum as a site of contact between political agencies and instruments and public experience and opinion was also a central focus for the creators of the museum because its short gestation period (less than two years) occurred in the heat of the culture wars that spread across Australia's national and cultural institutions in the 1990s and early 2000s and that marked the much more extensive gestation of the National Museum of Australia (which was conceptualized in the 1970s, enacted in 1980, and opened in 2001).[10] Not only was the Immigration Museum able to put a face to the experience and implications of racism (as per Bangstad's recommended strategy), but it was implicated in the attacks, targeted by anti-racist speakers, many of whom based their criticism of the museum on a paradigm that appealed to the reasonableness of everyday Australians on the basis that 'I'm not racist, but . . .'. The antagonistic nature of any public engagement with racism across the national stage in Australia has meant that in making a direct contribution to the study of hate speech, the museum's actions have been brave and complex.[11]

Book aims and chapter outline

There is a multitude of ways in which the Immigration Museum case study might be approached, and whilst a large body of institutional, collections, and exhibitions based analysis has contributed directly to the research undertaken for this book, my primary goal is to analyse the interaction between political decisions and policy development, institutional practices, and the broader social context and experiences (including racism) of civic multiculturalism in contemporary society. My focus is, as such, predominantly an institutional one that has been narrowed further by my attention to the use of language and discourse around racism and hate speech as produced by museums (specifically the Immigration Museum), politicians, the media, and the interaction between these instruments and the general public. This approach was designed because while there are clear connections between government decisions, museums (which are often associated with government apparatuses), and the broader social population upon which these forces act (Bennett et al. 2017), the Immigration Museum offers a case study that disrupts the easy associations between government decision-making actions and processes of social governance by *showing* the public and administrative practices through which relations of knowledge and power are composed and exercised. Indeed, the museum's first director,

Anna Malgorzewicz, has said – perhaps provocatively to emphasize this point – that it opened fundamentally with the brief of being a museum about policy, not people.[12] This statement reflects the fact that the museum was an outcome of Victorian state politics (and the personal priority of the Victorian Premier, Jeff Kennett)[13] as much as it was a reflection of national level multicultural policy initiatives, and broader public debates about the culture wars, immigration, and race in Australia.

My purpose here is not so much to focus on the role and impact of *cultural* policy on museums and organizational change, but to examine the intersections between social policy and museums and the public sphere. The museum developments I address have also been specifically associated with public policy initiatives at different levels of the Australian Government, and comparing the National Museum of Australia and the Immigration Museum illustrates the co-existence of different policy approaches within different jurisdictions. Viv Szekeres, former director of the Migration Museum in Adelaide, which opened as Australia's first migration museum in 1986, explains why it is important to study museums within the context of policy:

> It is always difficult to pinpoint the origins of change in a society as complex as ours, but there were two reports commissioned by the Australian Government in the 1970s that were seminal. They not only captured and described a prevailing reality but also had a long-term effect on the museum industry and on the wider society. The Pigott Report, *Museums in Australia*, was published in 1975 and the Galbally Report on *Migrant Programs and Services* was published in 1978. They were totally unrelated to each other.
>
> (Szekeres 2011)

The Pigott Report (Commonwealth Government 1975: 6) and the Galbally Report (Galbally 1978) each had an explicit impact on the development of the National Museum of Australia (Chapter 2), and their influence extended to museum development from that period throughout Australia, including the Immigration Museum. Despite Malgorzewicz's statement, even a cursory overview of exhibitions at the Immigration Museum suggests that the institution has tended to explore policy through people (likely to be recognition that policy is not faceless and cannot in fact be studied in abstraction from people).[14] Indeed, the museum has been praised for its attempts to represent the seemingly abstract subject of government bureaucracy and policy – typically associated with papers, documents, and statements rather than human experience – within its exhibition spaces.[15] Although this effect is probably most successfully achieved in *Identity: yours, mine, ours* (see Chapter 3) in relation to multiculturalism, earlier exhibitions also attempted to represent the structural and political underpinnings of migration processes, law, and experience. For example, *Getting In: Australia's Immigration Policies, Past and Present* opened in 2003 with the specific goal of exploring the processes of entry that migrants to Australia undergo and the bureaucratic policy structures around migration in Australia.

Indicating the tenor of *Getting In: Australia's Immigration Policies, Past and Present*, the opening wall-text announced: 'More than 9 million people have migrated to Australia since 1788. Countless others have tried and failed'. The exhibition (which is ongoing) traces the evolution of immigration policy in Australia in context of changing concepts around national identity to show the connection between migrant selection and the demands of colonial, national, and contemporary economies. It draws visitors into its narrative by including an interactive 'citizenship test' that invites visitors to take on the role of prospective immigrants and face an interview by Australian Government officials. The scripted interviews are located in three periods – the 1920s, 1950s, and the present day – and exhibition visitors evaluate the applicants' responses against the backdrop of prevailing policy. The exhibition has been particularly successful at suggesting the contradictory impulses at work in immigration policy, notably in the late twentieth century, when bipartisan support for multiculturalism coincided with a reduction in overall immigration intake and increasing controversies over the treatment of asylum seekers. The reason the exhibition was able to make 'an important and welcome intervention in public debate about immigration and refugee issues' (McShane 2006: 123) was because it did not represent policy as removed from politics, ideology (national identity), or personal experience. It was neither a 'paperless' nor a 'peopleless' exhibition, as Ian McShane (2006: 123–4) astutely argued:

> How can exhibition curators and designers convey the importance of documentation without papering the walls with departmental files? Conversely, to what extent can paperwork alone reveal policy nuance and bureaucratic attitudes? The exhibition responds . . . with vignettes of personal 'immigration stories'.[16]

This book progresses in the following way. My overarching framework is presented in 'It's a summer of sequels. The culture wars are back. So is the civil rights movement' (Cotter 2017), which introduces the institutional and intellectual framework within which the book operates and the conceptual model of the trilogy that I have adopted for the series to which it contributes. The current chapter outlines the key features of the argument that extend through the chapters that follow, and positions the study in context of the field of contemporary museum studies. The historical scope of *Museums and Racism* moves from the emergence of the field of multicultural policy from the early 1970s in Australia through to the current day, and it includes some of the public debates around racism that have occurred within and responded to political culture and events across this five-decade period.

Rather than attempting to be comprehensive (impossible in this short volume), I have approached the topic by bookending my discussion with a pair of incisive examples – that presents the institutional debates around the conceptualization of the Immigration Museum on the one hand, and that analyses the opening of its most recent permanent exhibition, *Identity: yours, mine, ours*, on the other hand. The first example that is discussed in this chapter, occurring roughly through 1990s up to 1998, was chosen primarily because of its clear representation of a specific political moment in Victoria (specifically an optimism around multiculturalism that clashed with the viewpoint of national politics and, to an extent, public opinion). The time period examined in the third example, 2011–2012, was chosen not just because of the Immigration Museum's development of the topical *Identity: yours, mine, ours* exhibition, but because this exhibition opened in 2011, the same year as a new national multicultural policy was released, which was followed by a new national strategy to counteract racism just months later. My approach to case study development has also been highly targeted rather than comprehensive, and I have focused on internal and inter-institutional discussions (and archives) to examine and highlight the interconnections between museum and exhibition development strategies with policy, politics, and public opinion that were common to all three of the scenarios I investigate. Focused on the comparative case study of the National Museum of Australia's opening in 2001 and review in 2003, Chapter 2 represents the broader national context and political opinion, which created a very different set of conditions than what was offered to the Immigration Museum. Analysis of the Victorian case study in context of policy debates around migration, multiculturalism, and racism is not possible without this contextual framework.

Scoping the field

'There is, of course, nothing new in the suggestion that museums are usefully viewed as machineries that are implicated in the shaping of civic capacities', said Tony Bennett (2005: 521), making the point that museums have acted both as 'differencing machines' and as 'facilitators of cross-cultural exchange' in the service of government priorities historically as well as today (Bennett 2005: 529). Each policy era has generated a corresponding museological approach to representing cultural difference in Australia (as elsewhere). The 'biological racism' era that was associated with the Immigration Restriction Act in Australia commencing in 1901 (and extending through to the early 1970s) can, for example, be characterized by the national museum model established in the nineteenth century that was closely aligned with the colonial enterprise.[17] From the early 1970s through the 1980s, the dominant public policy framework was multiculturalism, which recognized difference as otherness (defined in opposition to a white Anglo-Australian norm) (Australian Ethnic Affairs Council 1977; Australian Council on Population and Ethnic Affairs 1982; Office of Multicultural Affairs 1989) and was characterized by increased support for ethnic-specific community museums and the subsequent development of museums of migration and immigration.[18] Multiculturalism was transformed into social inclusion though policies associated with the UK Labour Party policy ('the New Left') in the 1990s that sought to encourage questions about the relationships between culture, national or post-national practices of citizenship, and levels of civic participation (and civic 'agency') in democratic societies (Department of Prime Minister and Cabinet 1999; National Multicultural Advisory Council 1999).

Heterogeneity and diversity became key features of exhibitions associated with museums adopting social inclusion and cultural diversity ideals or policies through this period globally, which influenced changes in the ways many museums reflected identity.[19] Examples of this genre include the exhibition, *Australian Journeys*, which opened at the National Museum of Australia in January 2009, accompanied by the assertion that cultures are not distinct, self-contained wholes, but extensions and expressions of life that have extended across territorial, linguistic, religious, or cultural borders, that have long interacted and influenced one another through war, imperialism, trade, and migration. The exhibition sought to engender positive feelings about people feeling at home across cultures, possibly in order to come to terms with the colonial pasts of many European nations as well as contemporary ideas about social justice. This phase of museum transformation attracted criticism on the grounds that it constituted a 'depoliticized representation of cultural diversity, shaped by a virtually unhindered mobility in which Australia's cosmopolitan connections seem limitless and unproblematic' (Ang 2009: 20).

Over the past few decades, an increasingly self-reflective museology has attempted to critically engage with historical and hegemonic practices of cultural representation, and the essentialization and exoticization of cultural difference (that in the case of migration museums often translates to a celebration of other cultures). Work by Bennett (Bennett 2005; Bennett 2015) and many others (including many of the references cited throughout this book; but for an overview see, Karp, Kratz, Szwaja and Ybarra-Frausto 2006; and Bennett, Cameron, Dias, Dibley, Harrison, Jacknis and McCarthy 2017) has shown how museums have contributed to the constitution of identity through the management of difference, where difference is defined, repelled, assimilated, marginalized, or denied (Whitehead and Bozoğlu 2015: 252) in the context of an overall and privileged white narrative, meaning that difference is determined and defined by a mainstream set of practices, techniques and devices that are applied to make the space approachable, knowable and 'sensible' (that is, 'governable'). National state-governed or affiliated museums have particularly been subject to this kind of critique, which can appear a straightforward one in the case of museums built in the mid-nineteenth century located in buildings that have formerly been sites of colonial government (for example, the Immigration Museum occupies a former Customs House), as well as for museums that receive government funding, and/or are recognized as a direct outcome or instrument of a particular state initiative or policy (in the case, for example, of *Australian Journeys* at the National Museum of Australia). There has also been an extensive body of work focused on examining the 'utility' of culture to government discourses and policy initiatives, particularly in relation to museums in the United Kingdom in the early 2000s (Message 2009).

The 'museums and governmentality' and 'utility of culture' fields of literature (for overview see Message 2006; Message 2009) have both learnt from and influenced the development of alternative, culturally specific, identity based, or agenda museums that attempt to tell a story on their own terms, through a frame of reference established by their own priorities. I have written elsewhere about the development of culturally specific museums in the United States (Message 2014), and others have also argued that these sites developed out of recognition that the point of view reflected by traditional museums has often excluded the experiences of culturally and ethnically diverse groups (Peers and Brown 2003). Mainstream museums were also perceived as places where objects associated with the histories of these groups were not being collected, and where the broad or specific stories of these groups were not being told though exhibits (Watson 2007; Golding 2013).

The National Museum of the American Indian is just one example within the genre of agenda museums to employ very deliberate language to articulate the museum as a reclaimed space of sovereignty (Cobb 2005), and represent itself as a hard-won product of demands for distinctly new ways of 'doing politics' A similar argument has been made by Viv Szekeres (1990), who traced the origins of migration museums to the community and regional museums that emerged across Australia from the early 1960s. She drew parallels between the development of community museums and the rise of identity politics within the public sphere; a growing body of scholarly work on race, ethnicity, cultural diversity, migration, and cross-cultural relations; and increasing self awareness by mainstream museums about their historically normalized practices of excluding stories and objects related to culturally and ethnically diverse groups. While the nomenclature is awkward, sometimes too narrow (risking interpretation as being exclusive rather than inclusive), culturally specific or identity based and agenda museums have often taken the goal of disrupting the singular or homogenous stereotypes represented in national museums, despite continuing to use (or repurpose) many of the characteristics of the public museums that they offer an alternative to.[20]

The challenges of defining museums of migration or immigration differ from those facing culturally specific museums because they cannot have a vested interest in representing a singular or specific culture or heritage. Their emphasis is usually twofold, and their commitment to exploring migration experiences and the influence this has had on Victoria (in the case of the Immigration Museum) aims to complement and contribute to contemporary understandings about cultural diversity (that are additionally shared by museums like the National Museum of Australia that seek to be broadly representative). 'Cultural diversity' refers to the demographic composition of society where people from many different national, cultural, ethnic, racial, and religious backgrounds live together as Australians. Three 'types' of museums – migration museum, culturally specific museum, and national museum – generally represent an interest in recognizing people from culturally diverse backgrounds and exploring self-defined and changing identity relations within a given national context.[21] Another difference between migration/immigration museums and culturally specific museums is that while they involve multiple cultural groups, they are not typically run by any single group or multi-ethnic cooperation, but by a better financed government institution (the Immigration Museum opened under the auspices of the Victorian state government) or independent organization (the Migration Museum in Adelaide opened to the public in 1986 under the auspices of the former History Trust of South Australia) (Szekeres 2011). These museums are usually politically invested and viewed as political agents within the public sphere. For example, according to Moya McFadzean, who worked at Museum Victoria from 1995 (curator Migration and Settlement) before moving to the Immigration Museum, the museum:

> purposefully inserted itself more firmly into community conversations about diversity, inclusivity, prejudice, and racism. Alarming statistics on the status of racism such as those published by The Challenging Racism Project in 2011 have only highlighted the need for 'socially activist' museums to tackle these issues.
>
> (McFadzean 2012: 18)

While the genre of special interest or agenda focused museums might be considered 'un museum-like' (McIntyre 2006: 13), partly because of their self-proclaimed political interest where it exists, they are not anti-museums, but seek instead to explore what an alternative museology might look like. This remit has increasingly informed the development of museums that exist within a mainstream national museum oeuvre (exemplified in the United States by the National Museum of the American Indian and the National Museum of African American History and Culture, on the National Mall in Washington, DC).[22] In the case of migration museums, criticism tends to assert that the physical 'separation' of a collection or exhibition space does not challenge or deter narratives of white nationalism, particularly in cases like the Immigration Museum, which is a 'branch' or campus of the larger Museum Victoria (parent) organization. These debates focus on whether separate museums consolidate the otherness of the particular group they seek to engage with and represent by delinking the main stories relevant to it from the stories told in the national museum (which might dedicate little or no floor space to narratives about migration, for instance).

One problem that has been identified with museological attempts to represent a 'cohesive' image is that singularity has been interpreted as homogeneity, particularly where the image emphasizes the success and inclusivity of the migration story over negative, more complex, or divisive histories. Personal identity and individual agency can be subsumed by or reduced to an essentialized cultural image that correlates to an ethnic (or other) group identity. The autonomy of the group here overrides personal identity, which restricts the extent to which a person can ever act as an individual (either within this frame, or in order to counter the dominant representation). This approach does not adequately reflect the reality that communities are shifting, intangible groups delimited by one or more identity factors, experiences, or geographical locations (Watson 2007; Golding 2013), or the preference of individual migrants not to be defined solely by any single aspect of their experience. An over-emphasis on shared (consolidated) identity also restricts the potential for communication across boundaries, a 'multicultural' approach to exhibition-making that former director of the Jewish Museum of Australia, Helen Light (2016), has argued can lead to competition amongst multiple immigrant groups for equal space in museum representations and in archives. This situation has been debated over the last few decades in relation to the place of community exhibitions in national and other large public museums that seek to be representative of a broad and diverse national cohort. The concern here is that community exhibitions 'cycle' through communities, which are represented for a short while and then disappear again (O'Reilly and Parish 2015; Message 2006).

Alternately, however, even attempts to individualize further can be problematic. For example, while McShane (2011) praised the Immigration Museum for making immigration policy 'human' and relatable by emphasizing its influence on personal stories (an approach consistent with Bangstad's argument), the museum has also acknowledged the risk that can arise from over-reliance on individual experience. McFadzeon has previously explained her concern that: 'The distillation of historical narrative down to purely personal stories can result in the creation of a simplistic narrative where the subject of immigration itself is reduced to a string of decontextualized stories that cannot be analyzed or debated' (McFadzean 2010: 74).

While Victorian Premier Jeff Kennett identified the establishment of the Immigration Museum as a resoundingly positive outcome for the communities it represents as well as for the Victorian Government, the museum's development process included much debate over the political implications of representing cultural, collective (group), and individual identity through a framework of difference. Maria Tence, Community Liaison Officer (and later Manager of the Access Gallery) for the Immigration Museum, argued that neither she nor the communities she worked with wanted a separate museum (Tence 2009).[23] They wanted their contribution to the nation to be emphasized within and integrated throughout the main campus of Museum Victoria rather than being framed as 'different', and in terms that could be seen as less central to the political heart and mainstream representation of the nation or state. Despite this preference being shared by many communities, Tence (2009) conceded in the end that the development of the Immigration Museum as a separate branch of Museum Victoria was a political win for the communities, even if its eventual form was more closely tied to a policy outcome than may have been desirable. In making a case for the benefits of government affiliation – at least in the case of the Migration Museum in Adelaide – Szekeres (2011) put forward the similar argument that social and cultural capital coming from government support 'and the fact that the government bureaucracy maintained a "hands off approach" enabled the museum to weave its way through the complexities of ethnic politics, enlarge its audience, and maintain its independence and momentum'.

Political critiques that focus on whether identity specific, culture specific, and cause based institutions represent enough of a challenge to normative conceptions of mainstream museums are typically associated with 'the new museology' of the 1990s/2000s (Message 2006). These critiques, like the museums they examine, frequently have a theoretical footprint in Foucault's work and have been developed out of interdisciplinary adaptations of anthropology, critical race theory, radical geography, public humanities, and public history. These forms of critical engagement promote and are often the result of agitation by community based activists, politicians, museum workers, and scholars, as well as everyday community members, for the return of cultural patrimony, improved representation, and a greater attribution of agency. Not only have the representation of these concerns become increasingly commonplace in museum studies over the last few decades, but they have also made significant practical contributions to the ways mainstream – by which I mean national and state – museums define and direct their functions. A related feature of this genre of critical museum writing has been attention to demonstrating the contribution that museums have historically made to conditions of structural oppression, including racism. This approach shepherded a self-reflective turn in museology that led to institutional forms of reflection over the role institutions may have played in historical injustices (Peers and Brown 2003). The main bone of contention here has been the contestation of 'official histories' by speakers who have historically been denied the voice or agency to address or contribute to these and other narratives.

An argument that is frequently made for specialist identity based or culturally specific museums is that they challenge homogenous images and narratives of cultural or ethnic difference and counter negative stereotyping of those groups in the media, to correct or question assumptions about cultural practices, and to bolster support for a multicultural ethos. However, specialist museums can also add to the universe of stereotypes circulating in the public sphere. Although the images put forward by museums that represent themselves as activist institutions are primarily positive, they consolidate the understanding of difference as something that is defined *in relation to* a mainstream that that is being challenged. The images continue to present activists as claims makers located external to the national narrative and apparatus of power. This means that even within a field of political action that has been expanded to include a greater range of politically empowered voices and agencies, museums (both individually as well as the categorical field) often continue to represent only a small selection of typologies from which people can choose to identify. 'To consistently see ourselves as enslaved or as historical markers of segregation', says Ravon Ruffin, 'perpetuates our existence as only knowable in opposition to whiteness'. 'I don't know if my psyche can handle being jolted between slavery and civil rights narratives', she continues (Ruffin 2017). The construction of black resistance (often symbolized in a US context by the image of Martin Luther King Jr.) has become one such 'acceptable' stereotype of difference that seeks to counteract the representation of African Americans through a lexicon of disempowerment, victimhood, displacement, and slavery. The image of 'good' otherness it presents is seen as having been 'earned' through service to the nation, and by its contrast with other more divisive figures such as Malcolm X and other more volatile images of African American political activism (see Heller 2017; and Chapter 3 of this book for discussion on an equivalent Australian case vis-à-vis Hage 1998).

While Ruffin calls for a decolonization of the museum institution on the grounds that 'it is not enough that we find agency in our oppression', it is also the case that it is 'not enough' that positive stereotypes are developed to counteract negative ones, even by the identity, culturally specific, or cause based museums that advocate for social justice and the claims of the people they seek to represent. It is not enough that museums declare themselves committed to social and political change in the everyday world if they do not first examine the assumptions upon which they are based and the position of privilege from which they speak (see Message 2018). Indeed, museums must, as Ruffin argues, consider ways in which they can themselves 'leave home'. In what is effectively a call for museums to adopt a critical distance and approach to examine their own actions and assumptions, Ruffin (2017) encourages museums to 'forego what we think we know – a sense of security wrapped into a tidy narrative'.

Although she is talking about a process of decolonizing national museums in relation to the historical experiences of 'people of color' (Ruffin 2017) at the National Museum of American History, her advice has broader applicability. This approach resonates with the approach that has been taken by the Immigration Museum, which has similarly employed a focus on 'leaving home', albeit in a literal and pragmatic as well as conceptual way (one of its core permanent exhibitions is called *Leaving Home*). A campus of the state museum, Museum Victoria, it does not have its own official vision statement, but remains, whether it acknowledges it or not, part of a public sphere that is directly influential in the construction of images and ideals of nationalism. That the Immigration Museum does recognize the responsibility and the obligations that go along with this civic function, and that it does not shy away from representing the struggles it has with giving voice to the historical legacy and current personal and collective impact of structural racism contributes to the value it has as a case study for this book and for society.

Methodology and approach

My analysis has been influenced by Susan Leigh Star's call for an 'ethnography of infrastructure' that is interdisciplinary and requires fieldwork that 'transmogrifies to a combination of historical and literary analysis, traditional tools like interviews and observations, systems analysis, and usability studies' (Star 1999: 382). Although Star's focus resided with information systems primarily, the framework she explored resonates for anyone working with complex datasets of information (including museums, archives, and collections), particularly those looking to analyse the structure 'beyond' the dominant master narrative voice that has historically not typically problematized diversity (also see Flinn 2011). I apply this model more fully in *Curatorial Activism, Archiving Occupy* (forthcoming) – where I investigate how to work with infrastructure that has broken down – however it is sufficient here to describe archives as 'a fundamentally relational concept' that both shapes and is 'shaped by the conventions of a community of practice' which, like infrastructure, exist both in their own right, and as a mere component of a much larger assemblage (that itself contributes to an almost limitless field of data beyond that). Finally, like infrastructure, archives can be indecipherable, and it can take 'some digging to unearth the dramas inherent in system design creating' (Star 1999: 377). Although it is not the intent of this book to get 'to the bottom' of understanding how and why decisions have been made at various times in the often organic process of producing and subsequently documenting the Immigration Museum, this framework has been influential in guiding the digging I have undertaken through a broadly contextualized political field as well as in regard to my topical museological case.[24]

While I am interested in the potential of archives, including collections, to be activist (and it should be noted that I am presenting the physical Immigration Museum and the archives surrounding it as both equally 'archival' and infrastructural'), to take on the challenges associated with redefining communities, uncovering hidden stories, and 'radical and oppositional history-making' (Flinn 2011), there are many other appropriate methods that could be taken.[25] The development of case studies that cross institutional and sectoral fields and employ action research approaches to investigate 'the epistemological, paradigmatic, and explanatory aspects of writing about and theorizing about migration in history, law and the social sciences' is a priority for many social science oriented disciplines (Brettell and Hollifield 2000: 3), and is increasingly becoming a feature of the humanities and arts. This approach was taken in relation to the Immigration Museum by the 'Using Museums to Combat Racism' project, for example, which ran from 2012–2015 through an approach that was interdisciplinary, cross-sectoral, often international, and that collaborated with communities and stakeholders. Concerned specifically with measuring impact, the project took a 'transformative action research' approach to investigate if the museum's *Identity: yours, mine, ours* exhibition could counter racism and increase acceptance of diversity amongst secondary school students in senior high school years.

'Transformative action research' was defined by that project as involving 'ideas, discoveries and tools that seek to radically shift our understanding of practices and leads to a paradigmatic shift in the field in question' (Mansouri, Tittensor and Armillei 2015: 61). A similar, although larger-scaled project was the European Museums in an Age of Migrations (MeLa) project, which ran from 2011–2015, and sought to define innovative museum practices that reflect the challenges of contemporary processes of globalization, mobility, and migration (see Whitehead, Eckersley and Mason 2012 and the work produced by an extensive list of collaborators, many of whom are referenced in their volume). Research techniques more typically associated with traditional museum studies priorities and outcomes (such as visitor studies, exhibitions, and program design and analysis, and so on) also contribute to broader cross-disciplinary goals, as the MeLa project demonstrated (but also see Gouriévidis 2014 and, in an Australian context, Hutchison 2009).

Sitting behind these interdisciplinary multi-actor projects and museum based research is an even broader base of contextual disciplinary knowledge that spans fields including archeology, anthropology, and history. Techniques used in one field often transfer to and are applied by others, particularly in a field like public history, where a range of methods for working with culturally diverse communities (and resources), and the challenges faced by culture specific museums (and programs such as community exhibition spaces) in engaging with communities that have traditionally been isolated by government institutions are also recognized as relevant and valuable (Abu-Lughod 1991; Thomson 1999; Teo 2003; Abrams 2014). The need for studies focused on assessing and measuring cultural, organizational, and institutional change within museum staffing demographics is also critical. For example, speaking about the relationship in museums of staffing demographics and the reiteration of structural racism in the United States, Fischer, Anila and Moore (2017: 23) say:

> The persistent and pervasive presence of structural racism in our institutions . . . is at the heart of the museum field's failure to diversify its boards, staffs, collections, members, and visitors, despite over a generation of effort in this area. . . . Coming to understand and recognize entrenched racism is a difficult and potentially contentious undertaking – but also a necessary step – if America's museums are to serve its diverse citizenry.

This issue has been an ongoing one in many national contexts, including at the Smithsonian Institution, about which a report called *The Challenge of Cultural Diversity and Cultural Equity* was released by the Committee of Government Operations of the House of Representatives (US Congress) in 1989. Concerned with the lack of diversity and equity apparent in the structure and staffing of the organization, the report referred to the institution as a 'virtually minority-free hierarchy' (quoted in Message 2014: 181). In terms of the Immigration Museum, this concern was addressed through rhetoric around 'community ownership'.[26] McFadzeon said that at the time of opening, the museum was conceptualized to encourage public ownership of migration as a universal story, which included recognizing that migrant narratives are 'not just about minority groups. That it was bringing British stories back in and acknowledging that they're migrants too' (McFadzean 2017; also see Chapter 3 for further discussion on 'public ownership').

Before embarking on discussion about the broader policy context around migration, multiculturalism, and racism within which the Immigration Museum operates (Chapter 2), the trends in museological development to which it contributes and its correlating attempts (discussed in Chapter 3) to play a role in the 'management of hate' (Shoshan 2016), I want to introduce the Immigration Museum through a brief account of the institution's pre-history, by telling the story of the proposal to develop the museum at Station Pier in Port Melbourne. Although the Station Pier museum was not realized on the site or in the form recommended, the documentation and processes involved in the proposal were influential on what subsequently opened at Customs House in Melbourne in 1998.[27] The processes around this proposal are significant for revealing the political support for the museum as well as the ways that museum staff grappled with the realities and perceptions of this government support, which was at times, something of a double-edged sword. My attention to these processes also indicates the methodological approach that I have taken throughout this book, which, influenced by Star's (1999) 'ethnography of infrastructure', has privileged identification and analysis of internal documents, policies, correspondences, interviews with staff, unpublished reports, and proposals and collections (objects and cataloguing data). I have identified this approach as a suitable way to examine the frequently referenced influence of multicultural policy development in Victoria and Australia on the Immigration Museum, which can be further understood in comparison with my contextual case study of the National Museum of Australia in Chapter 2, that had a more volatile relationship to government instruments and changing priorities through the same period.

What does museum mean to you?[28]

The development of the Immigration Museum was a consequence or outcome as much as it was a component of an ongoing political action. A symbol of political will and policy ambition, it extended the premier's vision[29] of promoting Victoria as a progressive multicultural state, particularly given the increasing debate in the public sphere about the value of cultural diversity and what it meant for Australian society in context of the growing support at the national level for right-wing politicians such as Pauline Hanson, who had entered Australian politics in 1996 on a platform of racist 'common-sense' (Chapters 2 and 3). It was also connected to a period of capital growth in the state, and the rejuvenation of Station Pier (and later,

Old Customs House) was a cog in the premier's plan for redefining Melbourne as the cultural and events capital of Australia following a decade of national (and international) economic recession.[30] The impetus for developing the museum was also related to observations of the need to increase understanding about migration processes and multicultural policy, which, despite increasing initiatives at national and state levels (Victorian Ethnic Affairs Commission 1995; Office of Multicultural Affairs, Department of Prime Minister and Cabinet 1992; National Multicultural Advisory Council 1995; National Multicultural Advisory Council 1997) were reported as being poorly understood throughout the 1980s and 1990s (Bailey 1995). Outside of the Victorian Department of the Premier and Cabinet, the proposal and subsequent development of the Immigration Museum meant different things, including for the State Museum of Victoria (which was in the process of undergoing organizational change to become Museum Victoria and was itself in building mode, with the new Melbourne Museum scheduled to open at the Carlton Gardens venue in 2000), as well as for the Victorian public, including the migrant communities that the museum sought to mobilize and gain support from. While there was crossover in debates in museological circles and migrant communities about the form and function of the proposed museum, both groups recognized the museum's potential to rethink cultural diversity in 'a way that contributes across society and not just in folk dances and music and food' (Tence 2009). This final section of the chapter will present a brief overview of the initial proposal and the reactions of Museum Victoria and the communities that were consulted through the museum's planning phase.

While my initial intention in developing this book was to explore the links between the ways the Immigration Museum and government policy approach cultural diversity in order to consider the potential the museum offered as a public space to host debates over complex cultural issues, my interest in the research kept returning to the 'behind-the-scenes' work that took place during the proposal and development phases of the museum. Rather than analysing the museum's opening exhibitions, I decided to open my discussion with an overview of the preceding development period to demonstrate that museums do not have ready-made answers for the challenges that they face. These struggles include balancing the claims of communities and the general public with the demands of government, expectations about what constitutes best or innovative practice amongst museum peers, and the pragmatics of the collections, context, and structures within which they are working – all in the context of a constantly changing socio-political field locally, nationally, and globally. Recognizing the process of problem solving that is so often invisible to museum visitors and scholars offers, I think, a useful resource for any attempt to fully understand the challenges associated with producing exhibitions that engage with issues including racism. I was reminded of this when I came across a folder of notes written by Moya McFadzean in response to a seminar that had been delivered by Michael Ames, former director of the University of British Columbia Museum of Anthropology, to Museum Victoria staff in 1997, a year before the Immigration Museum opened. McFadzean's notes, more than being a record of the seminar, present an astute and articulate outline of the challenges that the museum faced in meeting a complex field of often conflicting and always urgent goals. Rather than summarizing the text I quote from it at length to fully represent her thinking at the time:

> Intellectual dvpt has proved to be a complex balancing act: Trying to be inclusive without complete cultural representativeness; representing large cultural groupings while giving a presence to smaller groups as well; focus on immigration as a contemporary as well as historical experience; focusing on act of immigrating while also addressing settlement and impact issues. Exploring impact of immigration on cult landscape without implying that there were settlers, and then there were migrants. Positioning Aboriginal experience within all of this without bashing people over the head with the implications and without presenting Aborigines merely as victims. Waking the tightrope over cultural sensitivities, the realities of the White Aus Policy, providing frank interpretation of issues while meeting political imperatives for celebration. . . . But I don't think we are addressing issues around cult div and multic explicitly. Not, at this stage in the development anyway, are we entering headlong into current debates about immigration policy and race – diffusing prejudice and racism through democratizing approach, through inclusivity and diversity of programs and events. Safe approach but we could be far more proactive – yet we don't want to alienate and preach.
>
> (McFadzean 1997)

***

On August 6, 1994, a single classified column inviting expressions of interest to develop a proposal for an Immigration Museum on Station Pier appeared in mainstream newspapers and 'ethnic publications' across Victoria (outlined at Parliament of Victoria Legislative Assembly (*Hansard 52 LA*), March 2, 1995: 292). It said:

> The Victorian Government has proposed the idea of a museum which will record and interpret the immigration experience to Victoria specifically, and to Australia generally. We are now seeking expressions of

interest from individuals or groups to develop a proposal looking at the feasibility of establishing such a museum on Station Pier.

(The Immigration Museum Consultancy
Group 1994, Appendix A)

The plan to develop an archive and museum complex on Station Pier in Melbourne had in fact been hatched much earlier, as part of a call to preserve the oral and material culture of migrants (Parliament of Victoria Legislative Assembly, March 20, 1991: 287–8).[31] While the plan didn't get legs until some time after Jeff Kennett was elected Victorian Premier in 1992, discussions about it had extended back to at least 1987, when the Victorian Government accepted a proposal ('the Sandridge proposal') for the development of the Dockside area that included a Migration Museum. A concept study was completed in December 1989, and by the early 1990s the development had been made public (Parliament of Victoria Legislative Assembly (*Hansard 51 LC*), March 20, 1991: 287; Parliament of Victoria Legislative Assembly (*Hansard 51 LA*), March 19, 1991: 387). The proposed museum/Station Pier redevelopment[32] was addressed in State Parliament in March 1991 as being the cornerstone of a cultural renaissance that was widely anticipated at the time for its potential to generate jobs and build the economic profile of Victoria (Parliament of Victoria Legislative Assembly (*Hansard 51 LA*), March 19, 1991: 387; Parliament of Victoria Legislative Assembly (*Hansard 51 LC*), March 20, 1991: 287–8; Kennett in Alcorn and Davies 2002). It was a troubled proposal from the outset, however, because of a lack of consultation with Museum Victoria, ethnic communities and organizations, and a lack of alignment with multicultural policy development.

Debates in State Parliament about the proposal in 1991 expressed concerns about improving access and resources for State Public Records and archives, and speakers promoted the idea of establishing a framework to enable public donations and corporate sponsorship (Parliament of Victoria Legislative Assembly (*Hansard 51 LC*), March 20, 1991: 287–8). The proposal's recommendations built on a concept plan that had been commissioned by Sandridge in 1989, but which had origins in an earlier proposal to the government in 1987 to establish the migration museum on Station Pier, which was subsequently identified as a 'major tourist and educational part of the tourist component of the development' (Sandridge 1991: 2). The proposed museum was presented as a primarily commercial enterprise and urban renewal opportunity that would rely for initial funding and revenue from tourism and from stakeholders including community members (for example, people who had entered Australia through the Station Pier gateway),[33] as well as other site users and vendors such as TT Line operations cruise liners (who operated the ferry between Melbourne and Tasmania) (Sandridge 1991: 3–6). The vision proposed by the consultants at that time was more firmly in the realms of tourist experience and entertainment complex than a traditional museum focused on recording and representing historical experience. It reflected the economic situation of the day, as well as, to an extent, the museological trends toward 'living museums' and 'edutainment' (Message 2006). Aspirations articulated by the proposal were for the pier to become 'the national monument to migration', similar to the Ellis Island Immigration Museum, which had opened in New York in 1990 (Sandridge 1991: 3), and with which there had allegedly been discussion of a potential partnership (Perks 1991; Schwartz 1994; *Sunday Herald Sun* 1994). Other similar models discussed were Sovereign Hill in the gold rush town of Ballarat, in regional Victoria.[34] Other themes mooted for inclusion in the project emphasized the experience of coming and going that was the key feature of the Station Pier site (The Immigration Museum Consultancy Group 1994, Part 3: The Museum: 3–20). This theme – one focus group participant suggested an exhibition called 'Hello, Goodbye' – made a lasting impact on the conceptual framework that was emerging for the museum through this time:

> The migration museum needs to focus on the information, the sensations and the emotions associated with the process of migrant travel and arrival in a new land, rather than on the history of migrants and their communities once settled. The pier as a place of departure – during the Wars for instance – is also significant and should be reflected in the museum's activities and displays.
>
> (Sandridge 1991: 4)

The confidential consultancy brief 'to assess the feasibility of establishing a migration museum on Station Pier as part of the Bayside Development' was released January 21, 1991 (Sandridge 1991). Indicating that its primary intention was to build a resource for commercial enterprise, the brief named its primary clients as the Sandridge City Development Corporation and the Major Projects Units of the Victorian Government (MPU) (Sandridge 1991). The report was cautious to avoid duplicating the functions of the Museum of Victoria in relation to its interest in recording the social history of migrant communities, however, there is little indication of dialogue between the proposal stakeholders or authors and the Museum of Victoria.[35] Whilst neither the museum nor 'ethnic communities' were named as primary stakeholders in the report, it did, however say that its 'ongoing success would depend heavily on its associations with specific cultural community groups, the Ministry for the Arts and the Public Records Office' (Sandridge 1991: 6). This statement appears as little more than lip service at a time when Museum Victoria was establishing and staffing a Migration and Settlement collections area,[36] and collaborating with the Jewish Museum of Australia and the Italian Historical Society, Co.As.It., to develop *Bridging Two Worlds: Jews, Italians and Carlton*, a landmark exhibition that opened in 1992.

Indeed, on the same day that this brief was released, Graham Morris, director of Museum Victoria, wrote to Paul Clarkson, director of the Victorian Ministry for the Arts, expressing the Museum's 'considerable concern about the proposal', which had been 'assembled largely in ignorance of the programmes in migration and settlement currently in operation at the Museum' (Morris to Clarkson, January 21, 1991).[37] These concerns were specifically outlined as (*i*) a lack of consultation with Museum Victoria; (*ii*) a lack of consultation with the Ethnic Affairs Commission; (*iii*) potential duplication with the museum's programs and proposals; and (*iv*) concern that the proposed museum would become direct competition with the museum for government and private funding and resources. A final concern was that 'such competition will hardly give the community reason to be confident about a coherent policy in this area'; referring to the areas of multicultural policy and cultural policy at a time when public support for these was becoming tenuous in some contexts. Morris said:

> The Museum is further concerned that the proposal has apparently not been discussed with the Ethnic Affairs Commission. There are sufficient problems relating to the successful development of any museum, not the least a museum dealing with migration, without adding to them by neglecting the government agency response for that area of social policy. This is all the more acute because the proposal could be seen as operating outside a commonly-agreed cultural agenda in this area, and consequently detracting from it.
>
> (Morris to Clarkson, January 21, 1991)

Following consultation with Andrew Reeves (Deputy Director, Human Studies Division, Museum of Victoria) and Anna Malgorzewicz (who was curator of the new Migration and Settlement division at the Museum Victoria), Morris eventually provided provisional, cautious support for the development of the feasibility study (Morris to Clarkson, January 21, 1991), whilst strongly recommending further consultation and consideration (Malgorzewicz to Reeves, January 8, 1991).[38] Whilst a consultant was appointed to develop the proposal further (Parliament of Victoria Legislative Assembly (*Hansard 51 LC*), March 20, 1991: 287; also confirmed in Malgorzewicz to Reeves, January 8, 1991), further discussion within the museum's operational areas appears to have gone into abeyance during 1991, and media attention and discussion on the public record also disappears at this time.

The Station Pier proposal re-emerged in mid-1994, when the Government of Victoria initiated 'a new feasibility study to investigate the establishment of a "Migration Museum"' (Malgorzewicz to McCubbin, July 5, 1994).[39] Again, Museum Victoria had 'not been involved in a formal capacity to advise the Government, nor is represented on the [Migration Museum consulting] Committee' (Malgorzewicz to McCubbin, July 5, 1994). There was also evidence to suggest a lack of consultation with community groups, certainly in the lead up to the classified advertisement seeking expressions of interest.[40] At this time, the proposal was accompanied by a new origin story:

> The immigration museum was an idea put to the Premier and Minister for Ethnic Affairs, Mr Kennett, by the *Sunday Herald Sun* in April. Two months later, Mr Kennett established a high-powered committee, chaired by the Estonian-born chairman of Western Mining, Sir Arvi Parbo, to investigate the proposal.[41]

The Museum of Victoria did not submit an Expression of Interest, a decision that some members of the Museum's Executive Committee thought a poor one.[42] The museum was, nonetheless, approached by Hilary Newton (Manager, Museums Unit, Arts Victoria) on behalf of a newly constituted Interim Steering Committee (membership at Department of the Premier and Cabinet 1994). Newton wanted to know the extent to which the themes of Migration and Settlement were going to be addressed in the programs at the new Melbourne Museum (that was being developed), and how the Museum of Victoria saw its programs in relation to a proposed Immigration Museum. The Museum's response was sent by David Penington (President of Museum of Victoria Council) to Arvi Parbo, Chair of the Interim Steering Committee on September 8). The concise response was the following:

1   Migration and Settlement is a key theme of MOV.
2   Complementarity of programs needs to be ensured in order not to divide the loyalties of constituent communities and the museum-going public; such division will not assist the viability of either institution. Possible ramifications of dividing the loyalties of ethnic communities, upon whose good will both institutions will rely for ongoing credibility and appropriate program development.
3   The expertise for program development at the IM lies with the MOV. It is anticipated that the IM will draw, through necessity and choice, on MOV expertise and resources.

(Museum of Victoria 1994b)

The important feature of the Museum's formal response was its recommendation of two options for the consideration of the Interim Committee. The first of these was marked as the Museum's preference, and it outlined a way for the Immigration Museum to become 'essentially, a site interpretation on the theme of immigration' that would be accompanied by an orientation and resource centre on immigration history. It would have no extensive collection development or management features, no research facility or profile, and no full-scale program of events. The recommendation was for the Museum of Victoria to offer its expertise in exhibition development on a consultancy basis. The second, less favoured option, presented the idea that the Immigration Museum would become 'essentially, a full-scale museum'. In the case that the Interim Committee adopted this recommendation, the Museum's preference was for the Immigration Museum to come under a wing of the Museum of Victoria, where it would be managed as one of its campuses. The response made it clear that this way forward would also require a sufficient allocation of resources to be made available to the museum. It also required a clear governance model that would ensure complementarity of programs, and offer economies of scale in regard to the infrastructural requirements (Museum of Victoria 1994b). Feeding into this formal response were internal discussions about the proposal's lack of clarity on resourcing, as well as its lack of direction. In a departmental meeting, curators from the Human Studies Division articulated concerns about the proposed museum's status. Key questions were:

* Will it be a semi- (or fill) government agency, or statuary authority? Will it be enacted? Into what government structure will it fit? Where does it fit apropos the Museum of Victoria (MoV) and other related institutions?
* 'What is the IM? Is it a museum, with all traditional facets of collection development and management, and research, or is it something different, for example, an exhibition centre? If it does not have a collection development intention, how does it propose to come to terms with material with which it will come into contact as a matter of course?' (McCubbin and Malgorzewicz 1994).

In the final instance, the Museum's Executive Committee took these local discussions on board, forming the view, represented in Penington's letter to Parbo, that:

* The Committee *AGREED* that in responding to the Immigration Museum's Steering Committee's verbal request for advice that the Museum should state that it has serious doubts about its viability and that due to heavy commitments to the Carlton Gardens Museum it could not become involved without the provision of special resources. The spirit

of the issue is that the Museum of Victoria could conduct a feasibility study or provide consultative advice on a paid basis, but that it has a concern that without proper ongoing funding the Museum will not be adequately researched.

• The Committee *agreed* that if the Immigration Museum was to become a full-scale museum with its own collection etc. the Museum of Victoria would be capable of taking it on as another campus if it was fully funded.' (Council of the Museum of Victoria 1994).

Regardless of the concerns expressed by Museum Victoria staff, the model that was ultimately adopted was for the Immigration Museum to be 'a full-scale museum', managed by Museum Victoria as one of its program areas. In September 1994, an 'Immigration Museum Consultancy Group'[43] was commissioned to undertake an analysis of a proposal to develop a Museum of Immigration on Station Pier to assist the Interim Committee in its considerations on whether to proceed with the proposal. Drawing heavily on the 1991 proposal (Sandridge 1991), the recommendations outlined by the 1994 report had a lasting influence on subsequent concept designs (Cunningham Martyn Design 1998), and initiated many of the themes and approaches realized in the finished project. One significant change that was made in the interim period was in regard to the location of the museum which, by mid-1996 was identified as sharing the Old Customs House building alongside a newly proposed Hellenic Archaeological Museum (Gillespie 2001: 364).[44]

Conclusion

There is a great deal more that can be said about the process that occurred from this period up until the museum opened in 1998 (including, not least around collections development, stakeholder engagement, and the representation strategies employed within exhibitions and programs). However, I want to conclude my discussion by returning briefly to the question that I asked at the outset of this section: 'what does museum mean to you?' In the preceding discussion I gave an overview of what the proposed museum meant to the Victorian Government and to Museum Victoria, but it was not until the 1994 report that this question was really posed of a broader public audience. The questions asked were basic ('what, in your view, is a migrant?'; 'what does the word "museum" mean to you?'),[45] and it is difficult to see a direct correlation between the answers provided (evidence showed little support for a museum) and the report's final recommendations (enthusiasm for the proposal), but what is perhaps most telling is the fact that focus groups included only migrants or children of migrants (48 individuals). Although broader consultation did invite responses from a range of other organizations and governments (local, state, and national), this was still overwhelmingly focused on feedback from groups identified as 'ethnic' (media liaison approached 32 'major ethnic' newspapers and '8 mainstream newspapers (capital cities, national)').[46] The lack of directed consultation with anyone other than migrants or first generation migrants as part of this process reflected the multicultural policy era of the day, which still associated minorities with migrants (recipients of government-provided services), and which had the related 'unintended consequence of displacing the experiences of British and Irish immigrants from mainstream immigration history', which contributed to the public perception that 'immigration history was only relevant to people not of Anglo-Celtic origin' (Gillespie 2001: 364; Cunningham Martyn Design 1998).

Maria Tence (2009) similarly recalled that it was not until around the early-mid 1990s period that the Museum of Victoria started 'collecting in a way that allows communities to reflect their histories. And not just what the curators or the institutions say'. Although she was addressing ethnic communities, increasing curatorial attention to issues and people beyond the museum was soon accompanied by the realization that the museum needed to 'democratize' the migration story so that it was not just about minority groups, an evolution of thinking that reflected changes in museological thinking and practice (evidenced by McFadzeon 1997), including a greater attention to techniques of audience research. For example, in contrast with the practice in earlier focus groups, the conceptual planning processes occurring in 1997 and 1998 sought a more representative set of responses. Gillespie (2017) explains that 'it was probably the first time we [Museum Victoria] did audience – front end evaluation, some formative evaluation and had some focus groups and so forth early on. That shaped some of what we did as well'. Initial focus group explorations are outlined in the 1994 proposal (The Immigration Museum Consultancy Group 1994), whilst subsequent formative evaluation of the 1997 concept plan is described in Cunningham Martyn Design (1998), which built an audience evaluation report from this.

The formative audience evaluation carried out in 1997 represents a change – of the 27 individuals interviewed, 8 were described as first generation Australians, just 4 were second generation Australians, and a majority, 15, were "third or more" generation Australians (Museum of Victoria 1997: 4). The views of these groups influenced the museum's intent upon opening to appeal to both 'special audiences and broader audiences', and to 'promote our cultural diversity and resulting Australian identity'. These consultations informed the museum's central charter, which was:

> to explore the histories of migration to Victoria from the early nineteenth century, to be broadly representative, to demonstrate that we all

have a migration ancestry unless we are indigenous to this country, to represent the impact of migration on Aboriginal peoples, to and promote our cultural diversity in all its forms.

(McFadzean 2012)

This mission has come to function increasingly over time as a platform from which the museum seeks to engage visitors with its other emerging values regarding cross-cultural communication, and debates over complex and contested contemporary issues. Although it was early days yet, the work conducted behind the scenes through this formative period set the stage for later approaches to stakeholder consultation as well as an increasing awareness of and interest in probing the contributions and challenges that the museum itself makes to systems of structural racism, as suggested by internal discussions in relation to the *Identity: yours, mine, ours* exhibition that opened in 2011 and to which I return in Chapter 3.

Notes

1　According to Katharine Gelber and Luke McNamara (2016: 324), hate speech is a term that is widely used, but lacks a single meaning. They quote Bhikhu Parekh (2012) who emphasizes three defining characteristics. First, hate speech is 'directed against a specified or easily identifiable individual or . . . a group of individuals based on an arbitrary and normatively irrelevant feature'. Second, 'hate speech stigmatizes the target group by implicitly or explicitly ascribing to it qualities widely regarded as highly undesirable'. Third, 'the target group is viewed as an undesirable presence and a legitimate object of hostility'.

2　Nitzan Shoshan (2016: 16) argues that the management of hate is an exercise of affective governance: 'Its elaboration, experimentation, and performance fall under the dominion of the state, if we understand the latter . . . as extending far beyond its formal frontiers to include a host of institutional sites, discursive genres, and political technologies that propagate its ideological effects throughout the social'. This approach is consistent with Bennett's (2015) account of the contribution museums make to the governance of cultural difference.

3　Holland Cotter (2017) says:

'It's a summer of sequels. The culture wars are back. So is the civil rights movement. So is the Civil War. They were all in evidence in Charlottesville, Va., on August 12, when a protest over the planned removal from a city park of a statue of the Southern Civil War general Robert E. Lee exploded in violence. Two sets of protesters met and clashed: a battalion of white nationalists, neo-Nazis and Ku Klux Klanners and a crowd of counterprotesters, some with Black Lives Matter placards. Then there was a second explosion, this one on the internet, when President Donald J. Trump responded to the fracas, after a significant pause, with an equivocating message. He blamed both sides for the violence ("What about the alt-left that came charging?"). He pronounced Robert E. Lee the equal of George Washington. He praised the "beauty" of the Lee statue and lamented the loss of other Confederate monuments'.

4 While many media commentators described the events at Charlottesville as 'shocking' (Cobb 2017), others saw them as 'timesslessly boring' for their mundane frequency (Cunningham 2017). Bongiorno (2017) addresses corresponding events in Australia which coalesced on debates about whether 'Australia Day' should be moved away from its current date, January 26 (the anniversary of the First Fleet landing at Port Jackson in Sydney). The 'change the date' debates were triggered by the conflict and violence over Confederate statues caused by the Charlottesville incident, and by an article published by Australian Indigenous journalist, Stan Grant (2017) about how we might deal with the historical inaccuracies etched on a statue of Captain Cook in Sydney.

5 As argued in Message (2018: 4), 'the disobedient museum does not seek to progress an "anti-museum" stance, and it does not offer a straightforward rejection of forms of governance, discourse, or disciplinarity but instead is a project space that identifies institutional edges as potential sites of affective action'. In the context of *Museums and Racism*, this means a focus on institutional processes, policies, and the documentation of such. It means understanding that despite their claims to curatorial activism (Casey 2001: 9; McFadzean 2002), museums do not intend to function as objects of resistance, but as sites that can encourage reflexivity by revealing the processes around governance and social management and that this internal critique creates the possibility for broader social processes of engaged and critical questioning.

6 See Chapter 3 for discussion about ways in which the paradoxes over free speech regulation and protection have played out in Australia in the wake of the Cronulla riots in 2005 and in relation to the use and disabuse of the Australian national flag and symbolism around the characteristics of 'Australian-ness'. The Australian situation differs from the United States, which does not have laws against hate speech. Waldron (2014) explains that 'For constitutionalists, regulation of hate speech violates the First Amendment and damages a free society. Even as they boast of despising what racists say, free speech advocate defending their right to say it on the grounds that regulation of hate speech violates the First Amendment and damages a free society'.

7 For discussion of the 'far-right' or 'alt-right extremists' self-identified with white nationalism and white superiority who mobilized in support of Trump's presidential campaign, see Posner and Neiwert (2016). Trump himself referred to them 'as some rough, bad people, neo-Nazis, white nationalists, whatever you want to call 'em' (transcript of Trump's comments in *Politico* 2017). The terminology I have employed in general is in line with popular media usage, although the affiliation with nationalism in Australia is addressed in Chapter 3.

8 Bangstad (2017) argues that 'a mainstreaming of racist, xenophobic, Islamophobic and misogynist hate speech in the public sphere in the US accompanied the rise of Donald Trump during the US presidential campaign'. Also see Morrison (2016), and Soltas and Stephens-Davidowitz (2015) on the rise of hate speech in contemporary life.

9 Indicating the association with the Immigration Museum and politically progressive ideas about cultural diversity, also representing the idea that had become commonplace of museums as battle grounds, the Honourable Justice Marcus Einfeld AO QC finished his launch speech for the Immigration Museum with the statement: 'Succeeding in this endeavor involves no less than a battle for the soul of Australia, For the eternal sanctity of the human condition, it is a battle we must and will win' (Einfeld 1998: 10).

10 Local media reported, 'There is more conflict on the home front right now as the intensity of what has been called "the culture wars" increases. The National Museum of Australia is the immediate battleground' (Henderson 2003).

11 A section of this chapter is called 'What does museum mean to you?' in reference to a visitor survey that I discuss later in this chapter, and to reflect the book's focus on museological interactions with racism (see Chapter 1, notes 28 and 45). I have focused this short book on the Immigration Museum because of this case study's direct and proactive engagement with policies (government) and the personal and collective experiences of racism that are recognized in Bangstad's project. Indeed, asking 'what does racism mean to you?' is a key premise for the development of the museum's exhibition, *Identity: yours, mine, ours*.

12 'The brief was that the Museum was to be about the immigration process and not immigrants' (Malgorzewicz quoted in Henrich 2012: 211).

13 Reflecting his long-standing interest in these areas, Jeff Kennett was Minister for the Arts, Minister for Ethnic Affairs, as well as Victorian State Premier. Kennett refashioned the Ethnic Affairs Commission in 1993, which he renamed the Victorian Multicultural Commission in 1996. He took on the title of Minister for Multicultural Affairs at the time when the recently elected national government under Prime Minister John Howard was moving away from the term.

14 Furthermore, this statement about the promotion of policy does not reflect the work that needed to be done 'behind the scenes' by museum staff in relation to building collections that consolidated the museum's commitment to bridge-building between directive policy structures and the 'people' (a feature of The Immigration Museum Consultancy Group 1994).

15 The Museum of Victoria's focus on policy was articulated in the 1996 Collection Summary and Analysis for the Migration and Settlement division of Social History, which also stated future collecting priorities as being: 'the reflection through material culture of the evolution of government policy and public attitudes towards immigration – White Australians, assimilation, integration, multiculturalism, cultural diversity, contemporary anti and restrictive immigration trends' (Museum of Victoria 1996).

16 McFadzean (2012: 17) also addresses the challenges the museum had around the question of how to bring the bureaucracy of migration to life. About the motivations for developing this exhibition, she said that:

> 'Focus groups [had] indicated that people believe the Immigration Museum can play an important role in the debate of current issues – such as asylum seekers and detention centres. . . . There is a desire for in-depth "factual" information to provide historical and contemporary contexts to policy, drawing upon statistics, policies and original documents. Finally, people want to be able to change or maintain their own intellectual position on issues based on an even-handed presentation of information – there is an unsurprising suspicion of the veracity of the media, whereas museums seem to be viewed as offering balance and reliable information'.

17 The exhibition *Identity: yours, mine, ours* (see Chapter 3) represents this period by including archival sources pertaining to the passage of the White Australia legislation in 1901. One display quotes Reverend James Black Roland, member of the House of Representatives, who said: 'Let us keep before us the noble ideal of a white Australia, a snow-white Australia if you will. Let us be pure and spotless'.

18 In the multicultural era, the word 'racism' was recognized and utilized but generally deflected in favour of terms that emphasized the celebration of difference and service provision to allow migrants to maintain cultural links with their 'homeland' as well as full integration (rather than assimilation) with the white Anglo-Australian norm. Museums, particularly community museums, were seen as ideal spaces to meet these dual goals.

19 Ozdowski (2016) describes the phases of Australian multiculturalism according to the following categories: (a) Early multiculturalism – Whitlam's Labor government (1972–1975); (b) Ethospecific services – Fraser coalition government (1975–1983); (c) The mainstreaming of services under Hawke/Keating (1983–1996); (d) Citizenship and cohesion under John Howard's government (1996–2007); (e) Equality and justice under Rudd/Gillard governments (2007–13); (f) Social cohesion under Abbott/Turnbull governments (2013–).

20 The Immigration Museum has consistently demonstrated the importance of language and terminology. An early internal planning document explains, 'we have tried to use text as an interpretive technique, not simply as the major means for conveying information to the visitor' (Immigration Museum (n.d.). Also see Zable to Gillespie, June 30, 1998, discussing whether the 'tone' of the creative piece he was contributing – that was to be used as a script for Gallery 4 – was appropriate). Recognition of the importance of text in the museum context followed on from the way language was used in focus groups held in the lead up to the museum. As if illustrating the point made by Emma Cox (2014: 34) that 'categories of migrant are often, when it comes down to it, attempts to claim certain relationships with a nation', focus groups in 1994 showed clear preferences about the use of terms including 'Australian', 'new Australian', and 'migrant' (The Immigration Museum Consultancy Group 1994). The approach developed by the museum does not define terms but asks visitors how they prefer to be addressed and seeks to provoke discussion about how we define others in relation to ourselves.

21 According to Szekeres (2011), museums became:

> 'increasingly aware of the reconciliation movement and indigenous history in the 1980s leading up to the 1988 Bicentenary at the same time as they became aware of immigration and multiculturalism. Museums largely "sidestepped" the issue by creating separate exhibitions for Aboriginal people and for non-British migrants. However, after the year 2000, museums began to exhibit the ways in which migration has impacted on Aboriginal people and how Aboriginal people and their cultures have survived and contributed to Australian society'.

In practical terms, this meant that the Immigration Museum 'accepted views expressed by the Aboriginal community that Victorian Aborigines are indigenous peoples, not immigrants in the accepted meaning of the term'. The museum's focus is as such, on 'the arrival of immigrants over the past two centuries to a land already owned and occupied; immigration for indigenous Victorians has been a history of dispossession of their land and the continuing struggle to maintain cultural identity. Consequently the Aboriginal presence in the narratives is in terms of impact and survival' (Gillespie 2001: 364).

22 Agenda museums are built out of and promote direct engagement between culture and politics, often functioning across various grassroots and formal governmental stages and platforms (Message 2014: 37).

23 The same point was made by McFadzean (2017): 'There was a lot of that talk
about – there was that marginalization concern and about hiving off immigration
as a subject towards a specific museum. I think there was probably also concerns
about what the larger museum would mean for those community museums and
the – not legitimacy but the respect for the way they were telling their own community stories and how that would interrelate with an immigration museum'.

24 Message (2014: 20–4) discusses the methodologies for and challenges raised by
working with museums and correlating archives, many of which have also been
a feature of the current case study. Any limitations of this study are not entirely
due to archival gaps, but also reflect my own selection processes. Rather than
seeking to build a comprehensive study, my aim has been to profile a partial
period of a particular process to highlight institutional debates and activities
within a broader conversation about government policies about multiculturalism and public debates about racism. The wide scope of this task, and of the
field of resources has inevitably led to some exclusions.

25 Just as other approaches would provide valuable additions to this study (see
note 24), research into other archives would do the same. I have primarily used
Museum Victoria archives, but others that would contribute to understanding
migrant experience in Victoria include community based resources such as the
Archive of Vietnamese Boat People and the Multicultural Communities' Collection Project in Melbourne (see Light 2016). Similarly, a further research approach
could have traced the influence of community based exhibitions on the museum's
development, or that of influential exhibitions, notably *Tolerance*, which was
shown in 1995 at Old Parliament House by the National Museum of Australia
(before their new building opened on Acton Peninsula). See Chapter 2, note 7.

26 The 1994 Station Pier proposal says:

> 'A survey of relevant cultural institutions in Australia reveals that the cura-
> torial and other staff in Australian museums have tended and generally
> continue of be of British descent. Only rarely are staff from non-English
> speaking backgrounds. This has characterized the community programmes
> of institutions which have typically developed few links with ethnic groups
> (although pressure from communities and government policy in recent years
> has encouraged some changes in this respect)'.
>
> (The Immigration Museum Consultancy Group
> 1994, Part 3: The Museum: 3–29)

27 Customs House was seen as a suitable home for the museum because it was
recognized as a site of Aboriginal occupancy and an initial site of immigrant
arrival. Opened in 1876, its functions over time included customs collector,
import controller and confiscator, and arrivals and departures administrator
throughout the White Australia Policy period, which excluded immigrants of
non-European backgrounds, and placed strict quotas on southern European
immigrants entering Australia (Division of Programs and Research 1997) until
1973 (Malgorzewicz 2000; Museums Board of Victoria 2016: 6).

28 The Immigration Museum Consultancy Group 1994, Part 2: Consultation: 2–6:
'What does the word "museum" mean to you?'

29 Many accounts identify the museum as being a specific directive from the premier (Gillespie 2017; Malgorzewicz quoted in Henrich 2012: 212; McFadzean
2017).

30 Under Jeff Kennett the Victorian Government embarked on a program of major
civic works projects to 'revitalise Victoria's capital city and restore its cultural

and commercial dominance by the turn of the century' (Office of the Premier of Victoria 1993). Outcomes included the Melbourne Museum (2000), Crown Casino (1997), the Melbourne Exhibition Centre (1997), Federation Square (1997), as well as the Museum of Immigration and Hellenic Archaeological Museum/Old Customs House redevelopment (1998) (Rolfe 2012).

31   'For several years, successive governments have been discussing the feasibility of a (Im)migration Museum at Station Pier. The initiative is part of the Government's agenda' (McCubbin and Malgorzewicz 1994).

32   See Sandridge City Development Company (Sandridge) and the Major Projects Unit of the Victorian Government (MPU) (1991), hereafter referred to as 'Sandridge 1991'.

33   'The actual Museum would be funded through sponsorship and one suggested approach was that the [Victorian State] Department [of Property and Services] contact individuals who arrived at Station Pier for donations' (Malgorzewicz to Reeves, January 8, 1991).

34   'As to the nature of the "Museum", the consultant seems to prefer something similar to Sovereign Hill, though "with not as much history", and with plenty of interactives' (Malgorzewicz to Reeves, January 8, 1991).

35   The National Museum of Victoria and the Science Museum of Victoria amalgamated to form the Museum of Victoria in 1983. In 1998, the Museum of Victoria was renamed Museum Victoria. The name changed again (in 2016) to Museums Victoria. Previous name and organizational changes also occurred earlier in the institution's history. As the period I am concerned with covers a name change, I have referred to both 'The Museum of Victoria' and 'Museum Victoria', using whichever is employed in the source being cited (McCubbin and Ladas 1998).

36   Migration and settlement developed as a key thematic focus of the Museum of Victoria from 1990, in line with developing state government programs. In response to meeting with Robert Mammerella from the Victorian Government (Department of Property and Services) in 1994, Malgorzewicz wrote a letter describing the priorities of the museum and the rapidly changing museum sector:

> 'I was appointed to the Museum two months ago to develop a collection and research base that documented the history of migration and settlement in Victoria. . . . There has been much discussion about methodology and philosophical approach as well as direct action (in relation to attempts by Australian libraries and museums to redress the lack of representation of 'so-called "migrant" history' in their collections). The proceedings of the Conference "New Responsibilities" held here in Melbourne in 1988 would be worthwhile reading and I strongly suggest you get hold of a copy. It is a good introduction to what is happening in Australia and to some of the arguments as to how best we achieve the goals Museum and Library workers as well as community representatives have identified'.

Of her own work, Malgorzewicz says:

> I am working very closely with the many established ethno-specific Museums and Archival bodies in Melbourne and Victoria generally. I am currently developing joint collecting procedures with these bodies as well as identifying alternative ways of working with and responding to, the needs to ethnic communities. In the process, community groups are empowered and play a significant role in areas of decision-making, collections guidance and the selection and interpretation if materials. . . . I am always happy to

answer any questions regarding the documentation or systematic collection of multicultural heritage'.

> (Attachment 1, Penington to Parbo, September 8, 1994,
> Malgorzewicz to Mammerella, October 10, 1990)

37 Although the plan was to include the Museum of Victoria, and her name had been included in the draft as a project team member, Malgorzewicz says 'It will be interesting to see when this happens as we have been ignored to date' (Malgorzewicz to Reeves, January 8, 1991).

38 A confidential memo to Andrew Reeves confirms Anna Malgorzewicz's prior knowledge of the proposal, about which she says 'Despite what we have seen on paper . . . plans for a Migration Museum at Station Pier are still very much at the conceptual stage'. Also she says she had heard nothing from them since her October meeting with Mammerella (Malgorzewicz to Reeves, January 8, 1991).

39 The 1991 Sandridge study was tabled at the meeting, but 'it and its recommendations are not to be made public' (Malgorzewicz to McCubbin, July 6, 1991).

40 Malgorzewicz was concerned about the potential direct impact the proposal would have by implication on her work at the Museum of Victoria. She says, 'This proposal has received some publicity recently, and as a result, has caused considerable concern among members of Victoria's immigrant communities'. Of particular concern were the names of members of the advisory committee (Malgorzewicz to McCubbin, July 5, 1991). A day later she followed up the letter with a memo to McCubbin following a phone call with Hillary Newton, about which she said 'apparently the plan is to get the museum off and running and rely on "ethnic" funding to sustain it. Let them try!' (Malgorzewicz to McCubbin, July 6, 1991).

41 Despite the proposal's earlier iterations, Howe has been attributed with the idea in a number of *Sunday Herald Sun* articles including 'Taking the project to the people' (*Sunday Herald Sun* 1994; also Ballantine 1994: 7; Howe 2011). Also 'Hilary [Newton] is uncertain of the driving force – but, the committee is told it is the brain-child of Alan Howe, of the *Herald Sun*' (Malgorzewicz to McCubbin, July 6, 1991).

42 Draft minutes of a Council of the Museum of Victoria Executive recorded:

> 'The Committee raised their concern that the Museum did not make a bid for the feasibility consultancy. Some members felt that as the experts in the field, a bid from the Museum would have been appropriate, The Committee *NOTED* that Museum management had expressed strong reservations in regard to the proposals ability to be achieved and that a decision had not been taken to submit a tender due to this concern. Moreover, given that this feasibility study may identify the need for ongoing Government support it is preferable that this is undertaken by a neutral third party'.

> (Council of the Museum of Victoria 1994)

43 The 'Directorate' for the project' (i.e. the consultants) comprised Ray Andrews & Associates Pty Ltd, Peter Root & Associates (a Sydney based project management and museum development consultancy), Building Technology Pty Ltd (a Melbourne based building and design management consultancy). Other members are listed in The Immigration Museum Consultancy Group 1994, Part 1: Introduction (Background to study): 1–4.

44 Kennett confirmed in August 1996 that a Hellenic Archaeological Museum was to be one of Melbourne's 'key tourist attractions' in the lead up to the Sydney 2000 Olympic Games' (Farouque 1996; Gettler 1996). Museum of Victoria staff were unenthusiastic about the development of this 'sibling' museum (McFadzean 2017). Also note that the interest in the Station Pier concept never diminished entirely. It became the focus of an exhibition held at the museum from 2004 to 2008.

45 Ironically, most respondents did not rate museums highly as places that they chose to spend their leisure time. . . . To the question 'How/where do you spend your leisure time?' no-one mentioned museum visits (The Immigration Museum Consultancy Group 1994, Part 2: Consultation: 2–12). Similarly, 'There were lively discussions in most meetings on what the "museum" should be called, as the majority felt that the term "museum" was inappropriate' (The Immigration Museum Consultancy Group 1994, Part 2: Consultation: 2–3).

46 Although the consultation was geared toward communities defined as 'ethnic', they were thorough in soliciting views, as described in the approach taken in just one case:

> 'In order to better ensure that primary ethnic community groups and relevant organizations and associations had an opportunity to provide input into the feasibility of a Museum of Immigration at Station Pier, the Consortium wrote to 101 groups and include a background paper on the feasibility study brief. In this letter we invited them to submit ideas for the Museum. . . . A second letter was sent to this same group, inviting them to attend a community meeting'.
>
> (The Immigration Museum Consultancy Group 1994, Part 2: Consultation: 2–17)

2 Multiculturalism

My purpose in this chapter is to bring the debates about multiculturalism, museums, and citizenship that occurred from the 1970s to the early 2000s in Australia into a shared frame. Without seeking to contend that there was an explicit alignment between the transformations that occurred in each of these fields (or even that the debates were interconnected, although evidence suggests this was the case), I examine the role that public cultural representations of Australian-ness played over this period in relation to the National Museum of Australia. The National Museum was conceptualized in 1975, created by an Act of Parliament in 1980, opened in 2001, and was subject to a government-commissioned review of its exhibitions and public programs in 2003 (Commonwealth Government 1975; National Museum of Australia Act 1980; Carroll, Longes, Jones and Rich 2003). It was chosen as the venue for 'Australian Citizenship Day' ceremonies in 2008, and that same year started opening new permanent exhibitions redesigned in response to the 2003 review. The museum's key dates parallel the development and transformation of national multicultural policies in Australia. First mentioned by the Australian Government (by the Minister for Immigration, Al Grassby) in 1973, multiculturalism was presented in 1978 as a long-term government strategy to develop social institutions that would respond to an increasingly pluralist society (Grassby 1973; Galbally 1978). A series of discussion papers and policies pertaining to multiculturalism emerged from the 1970s through this period, including the following: *Multiculturalism for All Australians: Our developing nationhood* (1982), *National Agenda for a Multicultural Australia* (1989), and *A New Agenda for a Multicultural Australia* and *Australian Multiculturalism for a New Century: Towards inclusiveness* (1999). *Multicultural Australia: United in diversity* was published in 2003.[1] As the changes in policy indicate, a contraction of political interest in multiculturalism occurred during this period, and national agendas of the following period (1990s and 2000s) were subsequently transformed in line with a new global appetite for the 'soft' notions of social cohesion and harmony.

Figure 2.1 National Museum of Australia, Canberra
Photograph by Kylie Message.

This same period saw a re-evaluation of concepts of citizenship that was paralleled in changing ideas about museum practice that consequently came to be associated with contemporary museology. Much has been written about the historical allegiance of citizenship and national museums, whereby traditional nineteenth- and twentieth-century museums promoted normative approaches to nation-building ideologies and an institution of citizenship that sought to achieve civic and social reform of the urban masses that were defined in opposition to non-Western and Indigenous peoples (who appeared to be defined by and reduced to ethnographic representations of their 'vanishing' cultures). In contrast, the increasingly globally savvy museums of the twenty-first century are increasingly identified by their aspiration to contribute to the meta-narratives of civic unity and a common notion of public good by adopting advocacy roles, accepting ideas about the rights associated with 'cultural citizenship' and supporting or developing strategic partnerships with local areas and Indigenous and migrant source communities. As the overview in Chapter 1 showed, many contemporary museums (especially those that are national or government funded) endeavour to challenge the idea that culture and politics have a dichotomous relationship. In addition to their aim to preserve culture, they provide a place where culture and identity can be performed, generated, and recognized as dynamic and political. In many cases, this aim means identifying and critiquing the systemic framework of racism that museums have historically been developed within.

Such museums tend to exist within societies that are pragmatically multicultural, including Australia, Canada, and New Zealand. Contextualized by policy ideals that encourage migrants to retain and express their original cultural identity for the enrichment of their adopted home, museums in these countries are quick to recognize that this distinction can itself be a product of the social construction of migrants as 'people of culture'. The assumed 'otherness' of migrants and Indigenous peoples is what makes them culturally visible and, while this 'visibility' works to reinforce the invisibility of the dominant culture, it also narrows the citizenship options available to groups defined in opposition to the majority.[2] As such, contemporary museums increasingly seek to represent the complexity and debate about terms such as 'cultural citizenship', and some have taken on board Ruth Phillips' caution to avoid 'transmitting a falsely harmonious representation of conflicts not yet resolved in the world outside the museum' (Phillips 2003: 166). Thus, while contemporary museums invite us to recognize the continuing function of national government as a social (as well as political) act that affects people's lives in very personal ways, they also insist on the role of museums as technologies that can generate new forms of social interaction and a dynamic form of cultural politics. We can understand these changes to mean that the focus for many national museums in contemporary – postcolonial and multicultural – societies has shifted towards grappling with how to more equitably balance their service to diverse multicultural and Indigenous communities with their traditional commitment to government policy positions and civic reformism.

In Australia, tensions associated with the changing definitions, understandings and experiences of citizenship, museums, and multiculturalism were forced to the front of the stage in 2001, when the nation marked its constitutional centenary and when the National Museum of Australia opened in March as a feature of the centenary celebrations. The festive tone of the centenary was diluted by events that followed later that year, including the '*Tampa* affair' in August, the September 11 terrorist attacks, and the 'children overboard' incident in October.[3] A national election – which resulted in the re-election of the Liberal National Party coalition government led by John Howard – was held in November. We can understand that it was for reasons associated with fear and expediency as well as enthusiasm that an intensified interest in national unity came to characterize the political spectrum at this time. Although the subsequent 2003 review of the new national museum's exhibitions and programs was tied to the emergent history wars, the attack on the museum that was brewing at that time must also be contextualized against a backdrop of the rise of the new right globally and the radicalization of the Australian Liberal Party during the 1990s, which elevated 'political correctness' to a term of abuse and made anything seen as elite driven or interest group driven a target. In some ways, the assault on academic history and multiculturalism had as much to do with the general attack on the perceived process of policy and decision-making as it did with the issues themselves.

The overarching aim of this chapter is to present an overview of the political field and policy sector at the national level to contextualize my analysis of the development of the Immigration Museum in the Australian state of Victoria. It is not possible to fully understand the actions taken politically or museologically in regard to the Immigration Museum without having some understanding about shifting policy positions pertaining to multiculturalism and citizenship occurring nationally. As such, this chapter presents a case study of the period 2001–2003 in relation to the policy developments unfolding from the 1970s through to the late 2000s, to explore the ways that government-funded institutions, particularly cultural ones, have sought to provide opportunities for public policies and community attitudes to intersect and even become mutually informative. As other parts of this book argue, cross-sectoral and interdisciplinary influence and negotiation have been a key factor for the Immigration Museum in Melbourne. The National Museum of Australia functions as a comparative case study, tracing how a different set of national influences and political agendas impacted upon that museum's development, in and through dialogue with contemporary policy preferences, as articulated, for example, in the 1982 discussion paper *Multiculturalism for All Australians*:

> The dynamic character of multiculturalism naturally calls for changes, not only in attitudes but also in our institutions. This will not be easy and, according to an Australian expert on ethnic relations, 'it is not possible to change attitudes and minimise prejudice if the structural conditions which encourage them are maintained.'
>
> (F. Lewins quoted in Australian Council on
> Population and Ethnic Affairs 1982: 13)

Australian citizenship

Citizenship has traditionally been understood to refer to a legal-formal contract between a person and the state, in which individuals are granted rights to political agency and legal support for being socially and morally responsible. It has often been perceived as a core component of national cultural homogenization. Notwithstanding the prior rights conveyed by British subjecthood, the formal legal starting point for understanding citizenship in this country is the Australian Constitution (1901), even though citizenship is largely omitted from its terms. 'Citizenship concerned the drafters [of the Act] acutely and they made a conscious effort to exclude the term from Australia's foundational legal document' in order to maintain the authority to exclude non-British people – notably, Indigenous Australians, Chinese, and people from non-Anglo-Celtic parts of the Commonwealth (Indians and Hong Kong Chinese), who shared the status of being 'subjects of the Queen' (Rubenstein, 2000: 580; also see Rubenstein, 1997: 307).

It was not until 1948 that Australian citizenship was first legally defined by the *Nationality and Citizenship Act 1948* (Cth), which later became the *Australian Citizenship Act 1948* (Cth). Despite amendments being made to the legislation over time (including the insertion of a new preamble in 1993 and the 2007 Australian citizenship law reforms), Mark Nolan and Kim Rubenstein have argued that citizenship continues to be used as a device of immigration control and exclusion (Rubenstein 2000: 587).[4] The events and collateral anxieties of 2001 certainly caused a surge of opinion and debate about citizenship to flood the public cultural sphere. Discussion coalesced on issues of national security, the treatment and rights of refugees and asylum seekers, and the 'obligations' (rather than the 'rights') associated with the privilege of Australian citizenship more generally. The reframing of the *Australian Citizenship Act 1948* into the *Australian Citizenship Act 2007* occurred in the wake of these discussions, and the changes made to this legislation have provided a further opportunity and reason to scrutinize the way in which we define and understand citizenship in a contemporary Australian context (Nolan and Rubenstein 2009). One instance of the re-evaluation during this period was the 2008 Australia 2020 Summit, at which participants debated 'the future of Australian governance: Renewed democracy, a more open government (including the role of the media), the structure of the Federation and the rights and responsibilities of citizens'. Just a month earlier, a panel of public advocates and intellectuals gathered in Canberra to commemorate the sixtieth anniversary of the 1948 act and to debate the topic, 'Australian citizenship: is it really worth having?' (Commonwealth of Australia 2008; The Manning Clark House Weekend of Ideas 2008).

Constitutional law experts, including Rubenstein cited above, used this anniversary and other key dates (for example, the fiftieth anniversary of Australian citizenship) to call for a re-evaluation of definitions pertaining to citizenship in the Australian Constitution on the basis that the 'failure to engage properly in informed debate about citizenship' has been a key reason for the existence of stark differences between the formal legal status of citizenship (and inconsistencies therein) and the broader sense of the civic value of membership in the Australian community.[5] This insistence on the plurality and diversity of citizenship registers changing understandings of citizenship in public (if not government) cultures globally. It acknowledges that discourses on citizenship are increasingly influenced by growing recognition that the contested norms of conduct and citizenship are themselves impacted by power relations, by the improved understanding that citizenship is more than a legal instrument, and by the subsequent acknowledgment that its cultures and practices are fluid and diverse.

Universal and cosmopolitan human rights initiatives have also contributed significantly to the change in focus from civic to political and social rights, as has the renewed attention to culture (represented as identity, gender, sexuality, and race), values, and habits as potentially unifying and motivating. This is particularly evident in the United Kingdom, where concepts of social capital and community cohesion – both of which are understood to emerge from communities that demonstrate a shared vision and sense of belonging – have been presented in policy initiatives as features central to the reconfiguration of a healthy civil sphere (Civil Renewal Unit 2004: 7; Message 2009). As a consequence, singular meanings of citizenship in liberal Western democracies around the globe, including the United States, Canada, New Zealand, and Australia, have been challenged by claims for the acknowledgment of difference in and by mainstream cultures, and by calls for recognition of cultural rights that are based on claims of ownership of, access to, and the right to profit from information and cultural patrimony, the protection of intellectual property, and the development and expression of cultural identities via education, custom, language, and religion, the protection of heritage, and demands that cultural rights are an important way in which to create equity between different cultural groups in postcolonial multicultural societies (Delanty 2007: 68). The debate about changing concepts and definitions of citizenship in these countries was echoed in this period by their deliberation about whether to ratify the UN Declaration on the Rights of Indigenous Peoples (which was adopted by the United Nations on September 13, 2007 after 143 member states voted in favour, eleven abstained, and four – Australia, Canada, New Zealand, and the United States – voted against the text).[6] The UNESCO Universal Declaration on Cultural Diversity (adopted unanimously at the thirty-first UNESCO General Conference in November 2006) also influenced these changes insofar as it addressed the implications of globalization (notably, expansion of debates about the influence of cultural pluralism on social fragmentation) on the territorial, sovereign state.

This chapter is contextualized by events occurring through the first decade of the twenty-first century, and by the corresponding work of citizenship scholars such as Joke Hermes and Peter Dahlgren, who argue that 'changing sociocultural realities underscore the limitations of strictly legal-formal notions of citizenship; not least, for example, in the face of the social problematics in post-colonial multicultural societies' (Hermes and Dahlgren 2006: 259). Following the interest that Hermes, Dahlgren, and other scholars have in examining the relationship between culture and citizenship, I present a survey of instances that demonstrates the role that culture (as a government tool *and* site of contestation) plays in developing and exercising diverse understandings about what it means to hold membership in the Australian national community (see also, Rosaldo 1994; Ong et al. 1996; Stevenson 2006). To come to terms with the purpose and potential of citizenship in a contemporary Australian context, I argue, it is necessary to move away from the narrow legal definition of citizenship and instead focus our attention on the particular practices, cultures, and politics of citizenship that play out in everyday spaces – as well as through the museums, policies, and institutions that create or challenge dominant cultural imaginaries. This chapter's overview of the processes determining who is 'included' within the Australian polity can be compared with Chapter 3's analysis of the Immigration Museum's attempts to challenge the conditions of systemic racism that museums have historically contributed to and consolidated.

Identity formation at the National Museum of Australia

Contemporary critical engagements with citizenship and museums have centred on the re-evaluation of ideas about power, authority, and the dissemination of these ideas into the public sphere – a process that was exemplified by statements that the new National Museum of Australia was to be self-consciously postmodern, postcolonial, and pluralist in outlook.[7] Reflections about the recent history of the National Museum demonstrate the urgency through which the exchanges between politics, culture, and society were characterized at the close of the twentieth century as a time when, to quote Dawn Casey, the museum's director at the time of opening, the issue of 'Australian-ness' was 'being debated possibly more vigorously than in any other period of the nation's history'. According to Casey, 'We [the museum] accept from the outset that there will be disagreements about the way we examine historic[al] processes or about our very choice of themes and stories and issues' (Casey 2001: 9).[8] This statement reflects the recommendations in *Museums in Australia 1975: Report of the Committee of Inquiry on Museums and National Collections including the Report of the*

Planning Committee on the Gallery of Aboriginal Australia, the document that first called for the development of a national museum. Chaired by Peter Pigott (and often referred to as the Pigott Report), the report recommended that not only should the museum 'extend the front-lines of knowledge', it 'should enable curious spectators to visit those front-lines and understand how some of the battles to extend knowledge are fought' (Commonwealth Government 1975: 6). It is my contention that in the institution's aspiration to engage with the history and culture wars (that escalated from about 1993), and in its aim to heighten awareness of the contribution that ordinary members of the national community make to conceptions of identity and citizenship (as symbolic ideas and everyday lived reality), the National Museum of Australia sought at its opening to create 'a more widely shared and more widely available form of "the political" as moments of engagement, of "public connection"' (Hermes and Dahlgren 2006: 261).[9] The representation of 'the political' preferred by the museum at that time was one that is centrally tied to ideas about culture, and linked therefore to a supposedly more inclusive, civics based notion of citizenship (Dahlgren 2006).

My interest in this chapter is not to sift back through the well-known series of actions, recriminations, responses, or the wider social implications that followed from the museum's opening and culminated in the 2003 *Review of the National Museum of Australia, Its Exhibitions and Public Programs: A Report to the Council of the National Museum of Australia* (Carroll, Longes, Jones and Rich 2003; see also Message 2006). Instead, I want to focus my reflection on two particular aspects of the process through which the National Museum was conceptualized and then presented to the public that have continued to inform understandings about the social role and purpose of the museum.[10] My first point of attention is the intellectual framework or approach that was adopted for the new museum. Seeking to represent identity as unfinished and contested, contingent and continuously negotiated, national identity was represented as a work in progress to which museum audiences were encouraged to contribute. The contributions of audiences and constituents were enabled on the basis that the museum would function as a public forum that aimed to 'speak with many voices, listen and respond to all, and promote debate and discussion about questions of diversity and identity' (Casey 2001: 6). The second notable aspect is the decision to present the museum as an active agent in the emergent history wars. As indicated by recommendations made by the Pigott Report (Commonwealth Government 1975), the intention for the museum to adopt the role of provocateur was present before it opened. These intentions were clearly aligned with an implicit attempt to question old certainties (especially those relating to the history of Indigenous people) (Commonwealth Government 1975: 71, section 12.8). As early as 1998, Casey publicly commented: 'It is never easy for a publicly funded cultural institution to become involved in controversy, but that is probably inevitable if we are to do our job honestly' (Casey 2001: 9). We can understand that the museum, rather than adopting the position of distanced observer or neutral reflection, sought to provoke and challenge long-held ideas about identity and question what citizenship meant in this country. Casey's desire for the museum to enact a program of social change and political intervention was motivated, in part at least, by the less controversial aim that the institution should incorporate and demonstrate to the Australian public a self-reflexivity about the general historical complicity of museums in the colonial enterprise.

On the one hand, it is possible to understand the museum's provocative purview to be an affectation associated with the emergent discipline of new museology through which it was designed and articulated (American 'new museologist' Elaine Heumann Gurian was involved in the museum's development phase during the 1990s). Its aim, however, to be politically aware, responsive to contemporary events, and to represent the changing place of Indigenous Australians within Australian society was based on the initial concept of the national museum (as recommended by the Pigott Report, Commonwealth Government 1975), which outlined a bicultural museum that should concentrate on 'Aboriginal man in Australia; European man in Australia; and the Australian environment and its interaction with the two-named themes' (Commonwealth Government 1975: 4, section 2.11). Early exhibitions such as *Landmarks: People, land and political change* (exhibited in 1993 at the museum's temporary location at Old Parliament House, Canberra) presented the reconciliation project as a way to bring these themes into dialogue to make the museum appear contemporary and relevant.[11] The exhibition sought to improve the public's understanding of the reconciliation project, which had been formed largely through the media's coverage of events including Indigenous responses to the 1988 Bicentenary of the arrival of the First Fleet in Sydney (problematically promoted as the 'celebration of the nation'), as well as the 1992 Mabo ruling.[12]

Although commentators sometimes contend that the level of public interest in reconciliation in Australia was indicated by the great numbers of signatures (more than one million) that were collected in thousands of 'sorry books' and by the more than 260 local reconciliation groups that were established to mark the inaugural National Sorry Day held on May 26 1998, the majority of Australians did not sign sorry books or go on reconciliation marches.[13] For his part, Prime Minister John Howard steadfastly refused to lead or have any part in offering a formal national apology for past mistreatment of Aboriginal people, arguing that Australians should not be asked to 'accept responsibility for the acts of earlier generations, sanctioned by the law of the times' (quoted in Galligan and Roberts 2003).[14] Further, the

Liberal National coalition's electoral success at the 1996 national election was due as much to Howard's 'tough stance' as it was to his ability to tap into and reflect residual attitudes among the 'majority' of Australians – 'the battlers' targeted by his 'For all of us' campaign slogan (Hage 2003; Gale 2001). Even despite its varying levels of support, however, the reconciliation project was front of stage in the mainstream media and popular imagination in the period leading up to the National Museum of Australia's opening and the new museum, widely promoted as offering a 'public forum', was a logical site to host debates of national significance. The debate about reconciliation increasingly became associated with the museum when rumours started to circulate that the word 'sorry' was written in the Braille transcript that skirted the building's postmodern exterior (Devine 2006).

The prime minister famously responded to the new National Museum of Australia building by labelling it 'very un-museum-like' at its launch in March 2001 (*Canberra Times* 2001; McIntyre 2006: 13). His suspicion of apologies and postmodern museums was soon allied to claims laid by conservative commentator Keith Windschuttle that the museum's selection and representation of a biased 'people's history' overlooked the contribution of settlers and great Australians to the national project and misrepresented colonial events. Windschuttle derided the museum's commitment to pluralism on the basis that it gave 'equal time for every identifiable sexual and ethnic group' (Windschuttle 2001:16). His interpretation gained further traction when one of the National Museum's own board members, David Barnett – a former press secretary to an earlier Liberal prime minister, Malcolm Fraser, and Howard's official biographer – accused the museum of presenting a version of Australian history that was 'claptrap' and influenced by 'Marxist rubbish' (in McCarthy 2004).[15] Barnett contended that the exhibitions portrayed a revisionist 'black armband' view of Australian history that was politically partisan in that it championed 'unfortunates' such as workers and stolen children and ignored the contributions of 'founding fathers and prime ministers'. Of Label 0826–70, Barnett said: 'Heather Rose. Another unfortunate. The way to get a place in the Museum is to have something terrible befall you' (as reported by Morgan 2001. See also Macintyre and Clark 2003: 193). Despite the slowly growing public support for a national apology to be made to members of the Stolen Generations, Barnett took particular offence at the museum's Stolen Generations exhibit, denigrating it as a 'victim episode' (Macintyre and Clark 2003: 192).

Barnett's complaint about the National Museum of Australia's depiction of 'biased' accounts of Aboriginal experience and its concentration on the extraordinary achievements and stories of ordinary Australians (at what he considered to be the expense of notable Australians) stood in stark contrast with comments made by Al Grassby 30 years earlier (Grassby 1973: 2).

In a 1973 conference presentation called 'A multi-cultural society for the future', Grassby asked:

> How often do our television screens reflect anything like the variety of migrant groups encountered in a real-life stroll through our city streets, or particularly our near-city suburbs? The image we manage to convey of ourselves still seems to range from the bushwhacker to the sportsman to the slick city businessman. Where is the Maltese process worker, the Finnish carpenter, the Italian concrete layer, the Yugoslav miner, or – dare I say it – the Indian scientist?
>
> (Grassby 1973: 2)

Grassby's comments about the poverty of representation offered by Australian television were picked up by the Galbally Report in 1978, which lay the groundwork for the establishment of the Special Broadcasting Service (SBS) (Galbally 1978). The multicultural policies developed in the ensuing 30 years also led to the transformation of public culture in Australia. Initiatives such as 'Harmony Day' (established in 1999), the establishment of the Migration Museum in Adelaide (1986), and the Immigration Museum in Melbourne (1998), the development of cultural diversity policies by state museums and the leading professional organization, Museums Australia, as well as the establishment of the Australia Council policy on Australian arts and cultural diversity demonstrate that a significant cultural change had occurred, as do the many community development projects funded by local and state governments.[16] The national museum was also founded and designed during the early days of multicultural policy development. Refining the general approach outlined by the 1975 Pigott Report (Commonwealth Government 1975), the 1982 *Report of the Interim Council: Plan for the development of the Museum of Australia* envisaged that:

> The Museum will emphasise that Australian society comprises people of many different origins . . . pay special attention to events in the peopling of Australia . . . highlight the effects of cultural diversity . . . [and explore] how the concept of assimilation of new immigrants is being re-examined and re-shaped by pluralistic philosophies and practices.
>
> (Zubrzycki 2003)[17]

The report tasked the museum with enlarging perceptions of Australian nationhood and with providing a space that would invite public scrutiny of the policies emerging in the post-White Australia Policy era. It sought a museum that would enable consideration of the impact of such policies on the everyday experience of ordinary Australians. This was less a revisionist approach to history telling than one that sought to represent those people (Grassby's Maltese process worker, Finnish carpenter and Italian concrete layer, but also the diversity of Indigenous Australians) who had been previously excluded from the national register. It also recognized the role that museums had in measuring and reflecting (as well as influencing) public opinion.

From multiculturalism *for all Australians* to *Australian* multiculturalism

Multiculturalism was initially developed as a program of immigrant settlement and welfare support that aimed to assist migrants from non-English-speaking backgrounds to become Australian without jettisoning their previous cultural heritage. In 1977, the Australian Ethnic Affairs Council defined multiculturalism according to principles of national cohesion, recognition of cultural identity, and promotion of social equality (Australian Ethnic Affairs Council 1977). Advocates of multiculturalism represented Australia as being made up of people of diverse cultures that should be given equal status within the Australian mainstream, where Australian citizenship became the glue that bound these different groups into a national unity (Galbally 1978, para. 9.6, Kalantzis 2000: 99–111). This ideal was represented in *Multiculturalism for All Australians: Our developing nationhood*, which was produced by the Office of Multicultural Affairs in 1982 and chaired by professor of sociology and leading government advisor on multicultural issues Jerzy Zubrzycki (who was also a member of the Museum of Australia Interim Council responsible for the 1982 *Plan for the Development of the Museum of Australia*). At this time, Zubrzycki commented:

> The concepts involved in the legal status of citizenship are related to those of multiculturalism through the notion of Australian identity: the question of what it means to be an Australian in our multicultural society. An additional link is provided by the ideal of mutual commitment between citizen and nation – an ideal that is common to both citizenship and a cohesive multicultural society.[18]

Citizenship, the National Museum of Australia, and multiculturalism can each be represented as belonging to the fields of policy (political positioning and intention), ideology (philosophical belief), and/or pragmatic or everyday experience (cultures of citizenship). Each institution or concept responds to, reflects, and is implemented by one or more of these fields (which they can at times also seek to extend or challenge). Multiculturalism, for instance, can be readily understood as having three primary usages. The first is related to the field of policy, where it is used to direct the relationships and institutional arrangements between diverse cultural groups that affect access to resources, privileges, and participation in decision-making. The second usage, not always distinguished from the first, is related to ideology, where multiculturalism exists 'as a term for the philosophical basis for a culturally diverse society, i.e. the belief that certain institutional arrangements ought to exist' (Australian Council on Population and Ethnic Affairs 1982: 2). A third usage reflects the pragmatic multiculturalism of everyday life in Australia, as indicated by the goals asserted by the 1982 *Plan for the Development of the Museum of Australia* and by other evidence, including market research commissioned in 2002 by SBS Television, which found that, 'in practice, most Australians, from whatever background, live and breathe cultural diversity, actively engaging with goods and activities from many different cultures' (Ang, Brand, Noble and Wilding 2002). It is important to acknowledge that the third field of pragmatic or everyday experience provides more than just a context for the first two fields. Recognition of the lived reality and ubiquity of multiculturalism counteracts arguments that insist that multiculturalism is solely a political idea and public policy regime, and it allows greater recognition that claims asserting that multiculturalism is a 'top-down' project and 'the work of a small clique' ignore the reality of considerable demand from within the immigrant communities for improved services and status.[19]

Although citizenship, the National Museum, and multiculturalism can all relate equally well to each of the three areas just outlined, I have focused this chapter on the first few years following the opening of the National Museum because of its commitment to representing the everyday and non-constant experiences, benefits, and challenges associated with citizenship in multicultural postcolonial Australia. As a government instrument that invites participation by 'ordinary' Australians, it recognized its potential to inform or intervene in the further development of multicultural policy by providing representation of public sentiment about citizenship procedures and legislation. This intention was evident in the 1993 *Landmarks* exhibition, in which contested public opinion and debate about each of the three national landmarks was represented. A further example that demonstrated the museum's potential to provide a significant space for political advocacy (if not recognition or protest) was the agreement by the Yolngu people from Yirrkala, north-eastern Arnhem Land, to work with anthropologist Howard Morphy to develop a *yingapungapu* sand sculpture and performance as part of the National Museum's opening ceremony.

According to Morphy, Yolngu leaders 'saw an exhibition in Canberra as a means of continuing to demonstrate to a national audience their native title rights over the coastal waters of Blue Mud Bay' (Morphy 2006: 482).

The potential the Yolgnu saw for the museum to play a role in their struggle for land rights was reiterated by their subsequent preference for the hearing into their claim to be held at the National Museum of Australia (as a site they now felt a symbolic connection with) rather than at the High Court of Australia.[20] This example demonstrates that more than just offering a public space or forum, the museum provided an official platform for people to occupy in order to represent their interests to government. It also demonstrated a challenge to the authority of the traditional notion of citizenship as a legal instrument represented exclusively by the legal apparatus (the High Court). This relationship also indicates that the 'national' museum was valued by Yolgnu precisely *for* its ties to government and that this connection was understood to demonstrate governmental legitimation of the representation being made – at least symbolically. The cultural politics that motivated the decision to include the *yingapungapu* sculpture and performance at the National Museum shows that the museum was identified as a site of productive albeit contested understandings of national identity and history by players who had traditionally been excluded by national government policies. Furthermore, in continuing to promote the legitimacy of cultural forms and practices of citizenship, it showed the potential for the museum to become what Morphy called a 'site of persuasion' to counteract its traditional role as an exhibitionary complex or surface of government (Morphy 2006).

The intersection between the importance of the nascent National Museum of Australia as a symbolic national space and the multicultural policies emerging at the time were apparent in the 1982 *Plan for the Development of the Museum of Australia* as well as in the *National Consultations on Multiculturalism and Citizenship* report published that same year. Also chaired by Zubrzycki, the *National Consultations* presented multiculturalism as a 'live issue'. The report focuses on the pragmatically multicultural nature of Australia. To indicate (liberal) public sentiment in Australia in the early 1980s, the document cites an editorial feature from the Melbourne *Age* newspaper, which says:

> [Multiculturalism] is not a dangerous new 'ism' to be foisted on an unsuspecting nation. It is not a radical plot to change the nature of Australian society. It is not a devious attempt to open the immigration floodgates. . . . It is essentially a recognition of reality and an enlightened attempt to respond positively to the changes in a growing community.
>
> (Department of Immigration and Ethnic Affairs 1982: 3)

Like the *National Consultations on Multiculturalism and Citizenship* report, the 1982 *Multiculturalism for All Australians* discussion paper, as well as the 1989 *National Agenda for a Multicultural Australia* stressed the productive contribution that pluralism made to contemporary society. They advanced a social justice-cum-citizenship model of multiculturalism and argued that multiculturalism should not be limited to issues affecting minority groups alone. On the basis that they also recognized the currency of culture and diversity in the figuration of citizenship and national ideals, these strategies sought to have multiculturalism officially inscribed as a right of citizenship (Office of Multicultural Affairs 1989; Australian Council on Population and Ethnic Affairs 1982). Although there is insufficient space in this chapter to outline the transformation in policy positions that occurred from this point (see Chapter 3), there was a notable change in position after Howard's conservative government was elected in 1996.[21] Symptomatic of the Liberal National coalition government's attempt to regulate the citizenship contract between the individual and the state by reaffirming the productive connections between national identity and civic obligation, 'cultural' forms of citizenship and more liberal understandings of contributions made to an inclusive national community were no longer in political favour. Similarly, it was not long before the Department of Immigration, Multiculturalism and Indigenous Affairs was renamed the Department of Immigration and Citizenship, from which any sense of culture, let alone 'multiculturalism', was removed and in which distinctions between the formal legal status of citizenship and the more inclusive civics based notion of citizenship were reinscribed.

Unlike earlier policies that had centralized the language and concepts of multiculturalism and promoted the idea (reflected strongly in the National Museum of Australia's opening exhibitions) that Australian nationhood was 'developing', the national agendas of 1999–2003 relocated Australian-ness as a central signifier and marginalized multiculturalism. Apparent in the shift of terminology that moved to embrace the phrase '*Australian* multiculturalism', these policies stressed the adjective, presented Australian national identity as a fait accompli (exemplified by the great nation-building age of the 1890s) and asserted the critical roles of social cohesion and allegiance and responsibility to Australia over pluralism, which, particularly in the post 9/11 era, was identified as a source of social fragmentation. Designed ostensibly to 'update' the previous (1999) national strategy and to draw attention to building fears about social fragmentation, the 2003 *Multicultural Australia: United in diversity* policy called for the public to understand that strategies of social cohesion and tolerance were tied to issues of national security and social integration, claiming: 'Australians now see themselves as directly threatened by terrorism. In this context, community harmony and social cohesion are pivotal' (Department of Immigration and Multicultural and Indigenous Affairs 2003: 7).

According to sociologist, Andrew Jakubowicz, the Australian Government's continuing support for the Harmony Day campaign was closely aligned with the recentralization of a singular and unifying notion of Australianness within multicultural policy (Jakubowicz 2003: 9). While Harmony Day was initially developed as a program that would privilege 'mainstream' groups and stress inter-group harmony, it was refocused through the 2000s to balance out the post-9/11 'alert but not alarmed' advertisements developed as part of the Commonwealth Government's national security public information campaign (Jakubowicz 2003: 9). Schools, scout groups, and other civil organizations are identified as the primary target of Harmony Day, which effectively makes them (rather than governments) responsible for bringing cultural and ethnic groups into dialogue with 'mainstream Australia' in shared public spaces. Acknowledging the role that cultural difference was perceived to play in the 2005 Cronulla riots,[22] however, Harmony Day events contracted in focus throughout the decade. Continuing to reflect government suspicions about inclusive multiculturalism, they reasserted more traditional notions of citizenship based on tolerance and civic obligation, where shared but essentially 'Australian' values are reaffirmed.[23] Consequently, Harmony Day publicity came to promote a firmly depoliticized understanding of culture that evokes colourful concepts of food, fashionistas, and festivals (which echoes the 2003 Review's promotion of culture as an enrichment or add-on to the more fundamental Australian norms and familiar images of nation). Tied to its anti-racism and obligation-based agenda, Harmony Day today continues to promote the social capital and community cohesion arising from civic activity and community participation as a salve to the social fragmentation (read racism) that is perceived to have resulted from earlier policies of multiculturalism and immigration.[24]

Concern about the perceived ramifications of cultural fragmentation came to a head in 2006 when the national government proposed the introduction of a compulsory citizenship test to assess English-language proficiency and Australian civics knowledge and to require those applying for Australian citizenship to endorse Australian values. In November that year, Andrew Robb, then Parliamentary Secretary for Immigration and Multicultural Affairs, told a conference that some Australians worried that the term 'multicultural' had been transformed by interest groups into a philosophy that put 'allegiances to original culture ahead of national loyalty, a philosophy which fosters separate development, a federation of ethnic cultures, not one community' (Heywood 2006). Elite 'interest group'-driven politics was as much the target of Robb's conservative critique as the pluralist policies that were seen to endorse these views.[25] He went on to add: 'A community of separate cultures fosters a rights mentality, rather than a responsibilities mentality. It is divisive. It works against quick and effective integration' (Heywood 2006). These statements were preceded by Robb's introduction to the discussion paper on citizenship testing released in September, in which he encouraged new Australian citizens to adopt a singular national identity and represented this as the best way to achieve a sustainable national unity: 'Australian Citizenship is the single most unifying force in our culturally diverse nation. It lies at the heart of our national identity – giving us a strong sense of who we are and our place in the world' (Citizenship Task Force 2006: 5).

Ultimately, although *Multicultural Australia* promoted the collectivist ideal of 'unity in diversity' (as a phrase that echoed equivalent policies in the United Kingdom, the European Union and the United States),[26] it aimed to create a federated union that was inclusive of difference but only insofar as citizens demonstrated commitment to the 'framework of a uniting set of *Australian* values' (Department of Immigration and Multicultural and Indigenous Affairs 2003: 2, 6, my emphasis). Exemplified equally well by Harmony Day and the recommendations proposed by the 2003 Review, this shift is evidenced by the multitude of local 'multicultural' festival-style events that continue to promote national social priorities (cohesive national identity) and align multiculturalism with strategies for economic growth. Rather than being tied to community development as described by the principles proposed by *Multiculturalism for All Australians* in 1982, social cohesion as prescribed in 2003 by then Minister for Citizenship and Multicultural Affairs, Gary Hardgrave, promoted a 'unified' (singular) version of national identity in which national unity becomes 'our strongest source of national security'.[27] Critiquing a similar policy shift occurring in Britain at the same time, Jon Burnett contends that community cohesion had become a:

> euphemism for integration; and integration a euphemism for assimilation . . . while assimilation suggests a form of "hyper-inclusion" of certain forms of diversity, it also tells us equally about the forms of diversity that will not be recognized or accepted.[28]

The 2003 Review of the National Museum of Australia

In the context of the politics and anxieties generated by attempts to regain control of a nation-building program that was ostensibly 'Australian', it was unsurprising that the 2003 Review appeared at a loss when it came to actually prescribing or explaining how the museum might adopt its key recommendation to reframe national identity (and thus revisit its methodological pluralism). The review states that '[a] museum must . . . give some sense of the diversity of views, customs, and beliefs that occupy the shared cultural space that is modern Australia', and yet cautions against 'presenting an assembly of ill-coordinated fragments' (Carroll, Longes, Jones and Rich 2003: 7). Consistent also with Howard's commitment to avoiding using the term 'multiculturalism' at all is the Review's sympathetic evasion of the term. Of the eighty-six pages of the document, reference to migrants or immigration is made thirteen times, while reference to multicultural/ism is made just once – a mention of the museum's Multicultural Collection (Carroll, Longes, Jones and Rich 2003: 51). Given that the 2003 Review was widely seen as an attempt on the part of a conservative government to force an end to pluralist models of representation in favour of a more unifying historical master narrative, it was to the surprise of many that the review expressed cautious admiration for the Gallery of First Australians (although this response might equally have been due to a perception that the separate gallery distinguished Indigenous peoples as 'people of culture' in opposition to the majority, who were defined through their relationship with the nation).[29] On the other hand, the review members were dismayed by the pluralistic and multicultural approach to representing 'nation' that occurred in other parts of the museum.

The Gallery of First Australians had been designed as a large dedicated space that would recognize and enable Indigenous Australians to present their own accounts of historical events and experience in their own voices. The distinct space suggested a riposte to the exclusionist and assimilationist policies, mistreatment and marginalization of Aboriginal people that had tended to characterize relationships between Aboriginal and non-Aboriginal Australians. The Gallery of First Australians could, however, have been perceived as uncontroversial by the 2003 Review because the political rights discourse it embodied was not substantively carried through into the *Horizons* and *Nation* exhibitions, which were dedicated to representing Australian history since settlement. The only exception to this was the rotating theatre, *Circa*, which contextualized Indigenous claims for restitution against the dominant nation-building mythologies of the post-contact period. Demonstrating the growing public taste for reconciliation, *Circa* showed Indigenous and non-Indigenous people interacting in a shared public sphere and talking about what it meant to be Australian at the turn of the century. The 2003 Review singled out *Circa* for the most vehement criticism. It complained about its 'content and lack of coherence' (Carroll, Longes, Jones and Rich 2003: 17–20) and proceeded to offer a series of suggestions to improve it. In a letter to the *Sydney Morning Herald*, historian and former National Museum of Australia employee Ann McGrath observed that the 2003 Review represented an attempt to reintroduce into the national imaginary themes of 'great white bloke history' constituted primarily by 'Captain Cook and cricket caps' (McGrath 2003).[30]

In line with the conservative ideologies about tolerance and the underlying economic discourse of comparative advantage and nation-building that was favoured by the 2003 *Multicultural Australia* policy (Department of Immigration and Multicultural and Indigenous Affairs 2003), the 2003 Review of the museum called for strategies of representation that would re-centre recognizably Anglo-Celtic 'Australian' values such as mateship and the ability to extend a fair go to others, and sought to distil the museum's existing attention to pluralist and inclusive approaches to representation. It ultimately recommended that greater attention be paid to the economic contribution made by migrants and nation-building activities such as the Snowy Mountains Scheme to demonstrate the positive influence that migration to Australia had had on the great numbers employed by the project (Carroll, Longes, Jones and Rich 2003: 33). Similarly, it recommended that the museum deploy cultural diversity as a form of cultural add-on or enrichment:

> The Panel considers that more could be done to address the concern that the National Museum of Australia should represent the impact of migrant cultures on Australian ways and customs – from food, to architecture, to café streetscapes, and to footballers hugging in public.
> (Carroll, Longes, Jones and Rich 2003: 33)

The attempted depoliticization and stereotyping of culture strongly reflected the contemporary global backlash against multiculturalism that was sweeping the Western world after 9/11. It is also symbolic of how, in contrast with previous approaches that have seen 'mainstreaming multiculturalism' as a valuable project in economic and social terms, 'any support for multiculturalism on social grounds is now qualified, and conditional on its subordination to "mainstream" Australian culture' that is represented (in the recommendations put forward by the 2003 Review at least) by a certain national homogeneity (Nolan and Radywyl 2004: 58).

Re-evaluating Australian citizenship

Rather than 'languishing with the historians, the academics and the cultural warriors' (Rudd 2008), vernacular understandings and modes of expressing the idea of belonging to the nation continued to develop across the decade, regardless of (or perhaps resulting from) increasingly constrictive policy frameworks. This means that although the 2005 Cronulla riots and the assertions of jingoistic parades of Aussie pride that became a feature of subsequent Australia Days might be taken to evidence the contraction of an inclusive and pluralist public sphere, they can also, conversely, be understood to demonstrate that traditional understandings of citizenship as a normative legal instrument (divorced from everyday life) are being challenged within the public sphere, and to the extent that everyday Australians of different ethnic, racial, religious, sexual, and class identifications actively vie over questions about what it means to hold membership of a national community in a postcolonial multicultural society. Responding to the increased levels of public interest in the process of identity formation, and recognizing their role as social agents, museums across the country have also increasingly aimed to promote positive and increasingly liberal symbols of cohesive community based models of citizenship in which, in addition to complying with the basic citizenship duties of voting and reading the newspaper, individuals have the capacity to generate a healthy civic sphere through a range of activities, including voluntary contributions to welfare causes and participation in local clubs, associations, organizations, or interest groups.[31]

Rather than providing evidence of a decline of confidence in 'nation' as an effective socioeconomic and political unit, and rather than leading to questions about the continuing role and relevance of central government institutions such as national museums as sites where the nation has traditionally told its story, the conflict over identity that is represented by the 2003 Review and the events such as the Cronulla race riots demonstrate that any pairing of contemporary museums or museum-like activities or events with democracy now requires a consideration of citizenship as a changing concept in itself. This is vital because citizenship is the essence of a representative democracy that is accountable and responsive to its people and because, despite their association with governments, museums can represent a diverse Australian community that is defined by pluralistic backgrounds, interests, and positions. It is also important because in counterpoint to a decade earlier, when informal pluralism was one of the defining features of Australian identity, it was, by the mid-2000s 'harder . . . to be an Australian – an Aussie in a cultural, emotive, gut-instinct sort of way' (Teo 2006). Responding to the Cronulla riots in an article written for the *Sydney Herald Sun*, cultural historian and novelist Hsu-Ming Teo identified the tensions that continued to result from discrepancies in the way citizenship was defined, on the one hand, as a formal legal notion, and practiced, on the other hand, as a form of national belonging in the realm of pragmatic everyday life. She puts her finger on the challenge with her observation that 'Being Australian is more than formal citizenship; it is feeling like an Aussie as well. . . . A decade ago there were many ways of being Australian' (Teo 2006).

Conclusion

> I will be arguing the necessity of a robust politics of culture, a politics that is able to negotiate local and global differences. In this way, I am voicing a strategic optimism based on long-term possibility rather than a sanguine assessment of the current state of the nation. By moving in the direction of civic pluralism, we will be making a new social contract.
>
> (Kalantzis 2000: 100)

Although Mary Kalantzis argues in this passage for a 'post-national' citizenship for Australia that is based on a pluralist ideology, it is my contention that contestation over the 'national' has itself yielded new and complex understandings of citizenship in official and everyday contexts (even if the complexity has not yet been fully recognized in citizenship legislation). I want to conclude this chapter by reiterating my argument that the National Museum of Australia was not drawn into the history wars by whim or accident but that the curators and exhibition developers were led by the 1975 Pigott Report (Commonwealth Government 1975), by transformations in public policy, and by the transformations that museological practice was undergoing at the time to actively stake a position as a key player from the outset. Although no one could have fully anticipated the events that followed the museum's opening in 2001, Dawn Casey's comments about the need for national museums to involve themselves in public debate might, with the value of hindsight, appear to function more as a statement of intent than a mere coincidence or prescience. Not only did the National Museum seek to enact the role of socio-political agent and provocateur, it succeeded, albeit at great cost to many people involved, and with widely contested outcomes. Of greater interest is the seriousness with which the 'robust politics of culture' proffered by the museum was taken by proponents of the conservative ideology promoted by the government of the day. This means that the government and its representatives (exemplified by Prime Minister Howard) had a keen understanding that the National Museum's provocation, its demotic approach to representation, and its alignment with notions of cultural citizenship were more than rhetorical, and that the traditional utility of culture (where culture is an instrument of government) was being threatened if not explicitly inverted.

It is also interesting to note that the reiteration of instructive ties between national museums and legal formations of citizenship have continued to be reinscribed beyond the National Museum of Australia's opening and review. For example, a subsequent Australian Citizenship Day (September 17, 2008) was celebrated at the National Museum of Australia with a special ceremony. Having conferred seventeen people with Australian citizenship, the Minister for Immigration and Citizenship, Senator Chris Evans, declared, 'Australian Citizenship Day is an opportunity for all Australians to think about the changes that shaped our nation, and to reflect on the role we play in building Australia and our future' (Evans 2008). This 'cultural turn' was consistent with the official and emotional apology to the Stolen Generations made by newly elected Prime Minister Kevin Rudd, in February that year. While there is much that can be said about the apology, we can observe first the prime minister's pre-emptive strike against those who would interpret his words as part of a 'black armband view of history' and, second, note that it was a discourse of pluralism that framed the apology that also functioned as a rallying call to the nation to, in the words of Rudd:

> turn this page together: Indigenous and non-Indigenous Australians, Government and Opposition, Commonwealth and State, and write this new chapter in our nation's story together. First Australians, First Fleeters, and those who first took the Oath of Allegiance just a few weeks ago. Let's grasp this opportunity to craft a new future for this great land: Australia.
>
> (Rudd 2008)

The speech reiterates comments made in the 2000 report *Australian Citizenship for a New Century*, which eschewed any notion of common national values or shared culture in favour of public acceptance of diversity and abstract civic values. According to the Australian Citizenship Council, it is diverse values that underpin citizenship, and these together define and unite Australians (Australian Citizenship Council 2000). Should we, in this context, understand Senator Evans' actions as being a concession to the significant role of the cultural politics that have played out at the National Museum, or as an attempt to recoup the alignment of cultural nationalism and more instrumental understandings of Australian citizenship? I think that both this example and the earlier discussion about the Yolgnu community's use of the museum work to show that while the National Museum of Australia can be viewed as a technology that plays a part in constituting legal formations of citizenship (hence being the choice of location for the 2008 Australian Citizenship Day ceremony), its performance cannot be fully understood without a consideration of how it is shaped by the exercise of heterogeneous and everyday forms of agency (exemplified by the *yingapungapu* sand sculpture and performance). This means that the museum (and the history it represents), continues to be centrally implicated in the processes of identity formation in Australia – as intended by comments made by the Pigott Report (Commonwealth Government 1975) and reaffirmed two decades later by the institution's inaugural director, Dawn Casey.

Notes

1 Australian Ethnic Affairs Council (1977); Australian Council on Population and Ethnic Affairs (1982); Office of Multicultural Affairs (1989); Department of Prime Minister and Cabinet (1999); National Multicultural Advisory Council (1999); Department of Immigration and Multicultural and Indigenous Affairs (2003).

2 Of this process, anthropologist Renato Rosaldo (1989: 202) comments that 'the more power one has, the less culture one enjoys, and the more culture one has, the less power one wields'.

3 For further information on the *Tampa*'s rescue of 438 primarily Afghan refugees from a distressed fishing vessel in international waters and the subsequent events, and the 'children overboard' affair, which occurred shortly after, and in the lead up to the national election, see Burke, Brace and Jordan (2001); Megalogenis (2006); and Commonwealth of Australia (2002)

4 For information about the 2007 Australian citizenship law reforms, see Nolan and Rubenstein (2009: 36–8).

5 Rubenstein (2000: 578–9, 587 n. 65) cites a 2000 report by the Australian Citizenship Council as providing evidence of this tension. The report says: 'We must recognize the difference between citizenship in the legal sense and citizenship in the broader sense. That is why throughout this report, when the terms "citizen" and "citizenship" are used with a small "c" they describe citizenship in the broader sense of civic value of our society, relevant to all the people who live here. Not simply those who, under the *Australian Citizenship Act 1948* [Cth], have the legal status of Citizens'. See also Australian Citizenship Council (2000).

6 The Australian Government subsequently indicated its intention to rescind its position and endorse the UN Declaration on the Rights of Indigenous Peoples (*The Australian* 2009).

7 The pluralist approach was evident in early exhibitions developed by the National Museum of Australia (even before the new building opened on Acton Peninsula). To celebrate 1995 as UNESCO International Year of Tolerance, the museum developed an exhibition titled *Tolerance* (shown at Old Parliament House) that used items from the museum's migrant heritage collection (Zubrzycki 1995). In 2002, Dawn Casey defended the museum's pluralism on the basis that 'the world's newest museums . . . take a . . . many-stranded approach to national history'. She goes on to argue: 'We accept that there are few absolute truths in history. We admit many voices to the debate' (Casey 2002).

8 In a keynote speech presented to the annual Museums Australia conference in 1999, Casey said:

> 'The date of opening for the National Museum coincides with the celebration of a pivotal event in Australian history. Many Australians will come together to explore our collective cultural achievement through celebrating, examining and debating the 100 years since our passage into nationhood. I have no doubt that many in 2001 will also be debating the newly opened National Museum of Australia'

> (Casey 1999)

9 In tracing the development of the 'History Wars' in Australia, Macintyre and Clark (2003: 132–3, 220–1) argued that after he was elected to office in 1996, John Howard 'took up the prosecution of the History Wars [and political

correctness] with a vengeance', adopting the 'black armband' epithet employed by Geoffrey Blainey in his 1993 Latham Lecture (see Blainey 1993).

10   For a curatorial account of *Circa* and the *Australian Journeys* exhibition, which opened in January 2009 to replace *Horizons: The Peopling of Australia,* which was redesigned following the 2003 Review, see Schamberger, Sear and Wehner et al. (2008); and Morton (2008).

11   According to the catalogue, the exhibition attempted to examine land ownership through the lens of Australia's political history, and focused on three recent 'landmarks' – the end of the White Australia Policy in 1973, the Franklin Dam dispute of 1983, and the Mabo High Court decision in 1992 – 'that have challenged traditional assumptions about these issues' (National Museum of Australia 1993).

12   *Mabo vs Queensland (No. 2)* was a court case in which the High Court of Australia recognized native title and in so doing overturned the claims of *terra nullius* that had been used to defend British colonization. The *Native Title Act* was enacted the next year (1993), and in a 'citizenship promotion' speech in 1994, then prime minister, Paul Keating, said that pluralism:

> 'will guarantee an Australia which is not only culturally rich but socially cohesive and harmonious. Just as importantly, it will mean an Australia which counts among its primary values the capacity to find practical ways to mediate differences – not just ethnic or cultural differences but the differences between men and women, between urban and rural Australians, between Aboriginal and non-Aboriginal Australians. . . . The catchword is not uniformity, but difference. It is not conformity, but creativity. It is not exclusive, but inclusive. Not closed to the world, but open to it'.
>
> (Keating cited in Kalantzis 2000: 105. Also see *Mabo vs Queensland (No. 2)* [1992], HCA 23; [1992], 175 CLR 1 (June 3, 1992)

13   Sorry Day was established one year after the report of the National Inquiry into the Separation of Aboriginal and Torres Strait Islander Children from their Families was tabled in parliament, on May 26, 1997. See Human Rights and Equal Opportunity Commission (1997), and for analysis of the opinion polls published in relation to Indigenous affairs in Australia (including the 1991 establishment of the Council for Aboriginal Reconciliation), see Goot and Rowse (2007).

14   The intersection between the National Museum of Australia and reconciliation continued to be apparent. In their submission to the 2003 Review, for example, the Lane Cove Residents for Reconciliation wrote in support of the National Museum and its recognition of reconciliation as 'the defining issue of our nation'. See Lane Cove Residents for Reconciliation (2003).

15   Barnett's political persuasion was described in one newspaper article as 'far-right' (Mitchell 1999).

16   On the flipside, however, in 2003, Andrew Jakubowicz argued that 'the key institutions over which government has control do not represent the diversity of Australian society at all – the monocultural Cabinet (0/17), the monocultural High Court (0/7) and the monocultural ABC (0/7 government appointees) are the ones at the tip of the iceberg. Public representation on government advisory boards no longer has to reflect cultural diversity, where most participants are selected for their willingness to accept government cultural priorities' (Jakubowicz 2003). See also Australia Council for the Arts (1996); Australia Council for the Arts (1998); National Museum of Australia (2005); and Museums Australia (2000).

17   Also see the source document: Museum of Australia Interim Council (1982: 40, pars 1–35).

18 In Department of Immigration and Ethnic Affairs 1982: 1. See also Office of Multicultural Affairs (1989).

19 The claims are by Brian Galligan and Winsome Roberts and are discussed in Jupp 2008: 235. See also Galligan and Roberts (2008).

20 Howard Morphy, personal correspondence with author, 2008.

21 Although the policy change in Australia seemed to respond directly to a renewed 'threat' of cultural difference associated with events including 9/11 and with other local incidents affecting Australia and Australians, political consensus on multiculturalism had really been shattered much earlier. In 1986, Stephen Castles, Mary Kalantzis; and Bill Cope responded to budget cuts by a Labor government by publishing an article called 'The end of multiculturalism? (The view from Wollongong)'. See Castles, Kalantzis and Cope (1986: 4–5).

22 For details about the series of racially motivated mob confrontations that originated in and around Cronulla in December 2005, see Hage (2006).

23 Harmony Day is managed by the Department of Immigration and Citizenship as part of the Diverse Australia Program. It is celebrated on March 21 each year and coincides with the United Nation's International Day for the Elimination of Racial Discrimination.

24 In 1982, concern was expressed that 'questions have been raised' about whether the 'degree of tolerance, and even encouragement of diversity' represented in the discussion paper 'threaten national unity and social cohesion'. The text argued against this on the basis that 'Australia is strong enough to accept diversity'; however, it is precisely the same argument that came to be used by critics of multiculturalism in later years, from the 'one nation and one future' rhetoric of Howard's 1988 One Australia policy through to government responses to 9/11. Australian Council on Population and Ethnic Affairs (1982: 11). See also Markus (2001: 85–9).

25 The anti-elitist position characterized by suspicion about cosmopolitanism and political correctness links back to Howard's attempts to mobilize ordinary Australians as 'battlers'. See Flint (2003).

26 In his capacity as Chancellor of the Exchequer, just before being named British prime minister, Gordon Brown proclaimed the failure of multiculturalism in terms that were reaffirmed by the leader of the opposition, David Cameron, who remarked evocatively that '[t]he doctrine of multiculturalism has undermined our nation's sense of cohesiveness because it emphasizes what divides us rather than what brings us together'(Cameron 2007). The terms of this backlash echo the sentiments expressed by sociologist Nathan Glazer (1997) and others who have claimed that multiculturalism has failed and that the United States is fragmenting along ethnic divisions.

27 Hardgrave outlined the services of his government to recent migrants, which included distribution of the 'values-focused publications of *What it Means to be An Australian Citizen*' and a program in which 'migrants are taught about our national symbols, our laws, the significance of important days like ANZAC Day, our political system and even our national heroes' Australian Council on Population and Ethnic Affairs (1982: 14–16, 13), Hardgrave (2003: 11).

28 Burnett (2007: 355). Also see Castles, Kalantzis and Cope (1986: 5) who expressed similar concerns to the government's use of the term 'mainstreaming', which, despite its 'idealistic ring', might also mean 'that special services and institutions, designed to meet the particular needs of non-English speaking background people, are no longer required'. Their concern was that

mainstreaming might become a fourth phase in Australia's immigrant policies: assimilation, integration, multiculturalism, 'and now mainstreaming'.

29 Although the stories of Indigenous peoples were included in the *Nation: Symbols of Australia* Gallery, and the *Gallery of First Australians* did represent the political struggles fought by Indigenous peoples in Australia, historically and in a contemporary context.

30 It is of further interest that objects relating to Captain Cook (including a magnifying glass in a silver case and other navigational instruments) and cricket (a baggy green cap and bat belonging to captain Greg Chappell in the 1980s and a cap and gloves worn by wicket-keeper Rod Marsh in the 1980s) featured in *Australian Journeys*, which opened in early 2009.

31 For information about a range of community based models of citizenship that have been produced by or in association with museums, and for discussion about how these function within larger national and state infrastructures of policy and funding, see Message (2009); Morphy (2006); and Hutchison (2009).

3   Racism

This book is not about migrants so much as it is about the impact of national and state government policies about multiculturalism and racism, the process of museum development as both influenced by and a component of policy processes, and public responses to policy content as reflected by museums and the social world. As demonstrated in Chapter 2, I understand 'policy' to mean the instruments and technologies that progress a course of action through which forms of knowledge and power exert influence over decisions, actions, and other matters. My account is partial and while this is partly due to the intellectual agenda I have determined as appropriate for this short book, the corresponding approach to source selection I have taken, as well as the availability of materials, it also reflects the wider problem of 'the comparative lack of interest in histories of Australia as a nation of immigrants – by historians, by policy-makers, and by the general public' (Neumann 2015: 4). This absence provides a justification for Klaus Neumann's (2015) history of Australia's response to refugees, and it contextualizes the Immigration Museum's remit to represent the policies contributing to the everyday transactional reality through which relations between government offices and the Australian public have been directed, experienced, negotiated, and in some cases, resisted. The strategies employed in the development of Immigration Museum that I discussed in Chapter 1 demonstrate that museums (and the archives in which its internal institutional processes, policies, and decisions are recorded) are, like government policies, artefacts of knowledge production. However, understanding the range of museum actions and influences also requires, as Neumann (2015: 10) argues, 'the views of other contributors to the public debate: politicians, newspaper editors'. It is also essential, he continues, to:

> be aware of the fact that refugees and asylum seekers [and migrants] have not only been the subject of policies and public debates; they have also shaped these policies and debates – by turning up uninvited on Australia's doorstep, by articulating their interests or offering their

Figure 3.1 'Welcome' installation, Lynette Wallworth, *Identity: yours, mine, ours* exhibition, Immigration Museum

Photograph by Jon Augier. Image courtesy of Museum Victoria.

explanations for why they sought refuge in Australia, and as citizens who are contributing to a national conversation.[1]

One such contributor is South Australian Governor, Hieu Van Le, whose account of his experience as a 'boat person' forced to flee Vietnam following the war in 1977 has become one of the origin myths of multiculturalism in Australia. Often recounted as evidence of the success story of the emergent policies of multiculturalism that were developed through the 1970s, the narrative as he tells it paints a picture of a generous nation that had, under the leadership of Prime Minister Malcolm Fraser, 'opened the country's borders' to accept a higher number of refugees than had become the norm under previous governments (Stats 2015: 69). An unchanging feature of Le's charismatic retelling of the experience is the moment that the small fishing craft entered Darwin Harbour. Following a harrowing journey that had included unsuccessful attempts to land in Malaysia and Singapore before heading into Australian waters, the vessel's boat approached the nearing watercraft with both apprehension and hope:

> As our tattered boat chuck-chucked clumsily into the harbour, all of a sudden we heard the buzzing noise of a boat coming close to us. It turned out to be a tinny with two blokes standing in it. They wave at us and one of them held a beer, raised his hand and called out "g'day mate, welcome to Australia".
>
> (SBS 2014; also Le 2011: 7)

'Welcome' is a key concept in political discourse (Le is himself a politician). Even the speediest skim-reading of political speeches, statements, and policies shows the prevalence and symbolic value of the greeting and its association with friendship and acceptance for discussions about migration, cultural diversity, ethnicity, and multiculturalism in the forty-odd years since Le arrived as one of the first wave of boat people seeking asylum in Australia. And yet 'welcome' can also carry quite different semiotic associations and implications. 'Welcome' remains as much a privilege (rather than an entitlement) that can be offered, withheld, or rescinded as it does an invitation articulated with warmth. The distinction is illustrated by comparing Le's memory of the speech and actions of the fisherman in Darwin Harbour in 1977 with the reporting of events associated with the '*Tampa* affair' and the 'children overboard' incident in October 2001,[2] about which the prime minister of the time, John Howard, archly said: 'my friends, we will decide who comes to this country and the circumstances in which they come' (Howard 2001). 'Welcome', in other words, is always provisional and selective when applied by those in power; a political privilege reserved for those lucky enough to be designated as 'friends'. Rather than being the antidote to racism that is implied by Le's recollection, this comparison shows that 'welcome' is a symptom of structural racism that protects the assumption in Howard's speech that 'we' who are here first are entitled to determine who should or should not be welcomed and the conditions on which that provision will be made available.

This book profiles two key episodes in the life of the Immigration Museum: first, the planning process undertaken by the Immigration Museum in the years leading up to its opening in Melbourne in 1998, and second, the planning and opening of the museum's most recent permanent exhibition *Identity: yours, mine, ours*, which was launched in 2011. My discussion extends to include the earlier period leading up to the development of multicultural policy in Australia in the 1970s (a narrative and a process that is both aligned with and that has influenced the account given by Le and other migrants arriving through that decade), and the previous chapters outlined how, in Australia, policy initiatives around multiculturalism are created at different levels of government across national or Commonwealth, through to state, and down to local, jurisdictions. In Victoria, multiculturalism was a prime political instrument, and the museum was a key feature of Kennett's 'cultural renaissance' and attempt to rebrand the state as the cultural and economic capital of the nation. In contrast to the statements made by Prime Minister Howard, Premier Kennett pursued a proactive approach to multiculturalism, strongly opposed racism and xenophobia, and criticized the policies of Senator Pauline Hanson's One Nation party.[3] He was the first political leader to speak out against her maiden speech of 1996.[4]

Set against the ideological disagreements between Kennett and Howard, Hanson, and others over multiculturalism during the 1990s, the increasing current-day tolerance for and ubiquity of hate speech acts in Australia and elsewhere forms an urgent factor in the museum's ongoing development and continuing work, and makes this a timely study. Multiculturalism is central to this study because it was a structural precondition for the establishment of the Immigration Museum in Melbourne and continues to exist as a social 'norm' that is both associated with and contested by Australian civic nationalism (Australian Government 2017). Language, including the articulation of the impact of racism and race hate speech, is a key element of political as well as public discourse and this chapter explores how the Immigration Museum's exhibition *Identity: yours, mine, ours* seeks to navigate a complex linguistic field, which in turn is also both influenced by and impacts upon multicultural policy and social trends, as well as individual and collective life experiences.

Civic nationalism

Moving from a linguistic comparison of speeches by Le and Howard to a spatial one allows us to understand that Le's experience of being welcomed occurred at the very marginal boundary or edge of 'the nation' (as his boat entered Australian waters) in contrast with Howard, who, as Australian prime minister, occupied the political and symbolic heart of the nation when he spoke. However, the Australian public sphere is not homogenous, singular, or even particularly straightforward. It exists somewhere between the highly charged symbolic places of outside and inside, and was the space chosen by Adelaide artist, Peter Drew, to locate his 'Real Australians Say Welcome' poster campaign. Throughout 2015, Drew designed and pasted a thousand or so posters with the slogan 'Real Australians say welcome' on public walls and surfaces across Australia. The posters, designed to 'celebrate our multiculturalism' (Drew 2017), were created as a response to Australia's treatment of asylum seekers and the 'Stop the Boats' election slogan used by then Prime Minister Tony Abbott in the 2013 national election. Like Le's narrative, they sought to humanize the stereotype of 'the refugee' (by bringing it from the nation's edge into proximity). In drawing on the abstract symbolic imaginary of what a 'real Australian' looks like (in contrast with the 'un-Australian' term popularized through the 1990s by Howard and Hanson and applied to all range of people, including asylum seekers, Asian immigrants and protesters, *Sydney Morning Herald* 2005), they aimed to both show and bridge the paradox implicit within the term 'welcome', where one party gives and the other receives this greeting as a privilege.[5] The 'Real Australians' campaign embodied a preference for theories of civic nationalism that challenge the 'naturalness' of any historical connections between national identity, race, and colour in favour of service to the nation.

A year after Drew's 2015 'Real Australians Say Welcome' campaign burst onto urban surfaces across the country, the artist made and pasted up another set of posters. This time the posters featured the word 'Aussie' beneath photographs of Australians of different ethnicities from the eighteenth and nineteenth centuries. The series sought to 'embrace our neglected histories and expand Australia's identity' by challenging mythologies and stereotypes of Australian national identity. It did so by building a narrative around a 1916 photograph of Punjab hawker, Monga Khan, who applied for an exemption to the White Australia policy.[6] A third related poster series came soon after in 2017. It was designed similarly to the first two series, and also funded through crowd-funding sources. This time featuring the slogan, 'Real Australians Seek Welcome', it extended the message that Australia has always been multicultural by showing the diversity of Aboriginal language and culture groups that pre-existed colonization (Smith 2017). According to the artist:

> 'Real Australians Seek Welcome' is a deliberate flip of the original slogan ('Real Australians Say Welcome') because I think that in order to have the right to say 'welcome' we also need to seek welcome from other Australians, especially the traditional owners of this land.
>
> (Drew 2017)

Drew's graphically arresting posters have become popular features of social media feeds and the walls of Australian cities and towns alike. Public support has translated to financial donations via crowdsourcing campaigns (the first campaign raised over $8,000 within a short time of being launched), and political support for the work has taken the form of photographic representations of Australian politicians at Parliament House with Drew and his posters ('Real Australians Say Welcome') during National Refugee Week 2016. Directly adapting the language of Drew's iconic posters, the Refugee Council of Australia initiated an 'Australia says "Welcome"' program, and the campaign was featured on Melbourne's Asylum Seeker Resource Centre Facebook page on April 21 2015 (from which it was shared 260 times and received over 4.9 million 'likes') (Refugee Council of Australia nd; Asylum Seeker Resource Centre 2015). The 'Real Australians Seek Welcome' campaign was also affiliated with and supported by the South Australian Museum which took to social media on Australia Day, January 26, 2017, with the message 'We are proud to get behind Peter Drew Arts new campaign' (South Australian Museum 2017).

Indicating their propensity for attracting knee-jerk reactions (yes OR no) rather than considered responses, the posters have also attracted negative attention and vandalism. There have been several prominent cases of Drew's posters being vandalized or parodied (Samuels 2016; Di Stefano 2016). While the most frequent form of defacing has been through the addition of the word 'not' above the 'Aussie' on the poster (Gupta 2017), instances in Darwin and Sydney have been reported where the 'word "Aussie" has been torn off the bottom section of the poster and replaced with the words "Muslim Terrorist".' (Howie and Roberts 2016).

Between the warm political support extended to Drew's campaigns by marginally left-of-centre politicians on the one hand, and the hostile racist often white nationalist activism motivating the vandalism of his posters on the other hand, exists a diverse demographic field that encompasses a broad spectrum of political views. Despite attracting media attention for the extremities of the messaging (which may also be a response to the street based location and format of his work on the grounds that it 'defaces' the surface it is pasted onto), the 'Real Australians' campaigns fundamentally articulate a politically moderate moral message of equality and human rights. That the posters were usually pasted up in central urban spaces (frequently papered with political street art paste-ups and the like) suggests that their message was primarily designed for and consumed by viewers of a similar moral propensity. In other words, the posters (both the slogans and their locations) work from the starting point that they articulate the viewpoint of the moral majority and position any extremist reactions as outliers to this self-generated 'norm'. Indeed, while Drew has been called 'the poster boy for the silent majority in the middle' (Smith 2017), his 'silent majority' is not the middle-class 'Aussie battlers' invoked by John Howard in the lead up to his comprehensive national election win in 1996.[7] Drew's silent majority sought to represent quite a different cohort: 'the people who want unity and harmony but whose views are too often drowned out by the noise made by the far left and the far right' (Smith 2017).

There is little question that 'the middle' is an advantageous place to be, particularly if you share a majority opinion, and even more if you have authority to speak on behalf of others who enjoy positions of power (as the selfies taken by Australian politicians with Drew would appear to indicate). Moreover, even if culturally and politically diverse and characterized by heterogeneous life views, this 'silent majority' does not lack political influence and is (usually) financially stable with access to basic services such as education and housing. It is, as such, incongruous to represent middle Australians, who typically gain representation in the Australian Parliament through the electoral process, and who typically have access to basic human services and rights, as being disadvantaged, as the reference to them as 'silent' suggests. Moreover, despite media coverage of Drew as 'speaking up as loud as he can on behalf of those who remain silent because conversations around Australia's multiculturalism have become all too poisonous' (Smith 2017), the individual rights and entitlements of people within this majority are not, by and large, threatened on a daily basis, as are the rights and entitlements of asylum seekers and the other minority groups represented by Drew's campaigns and the advocacy and support organizations which have adopted his campaigns. This disjunct raises questions about who Drew's posters are speaking to, and who they are speaking for.[8] It also raises questions about the public appetite for multiculturalism – a much broader discussion that I will return to in a later section of in this chapter.

Wake up Australia[9]

While critical engagements with Drew's campaigns represent ideologically differentiated viewpoints, they have tended to raise similar questions about the campaign's representation of race, multiculturalism, and civic nationalism. Civic nationalism promotes service to the nation as being a better indicator of being authentically 'Australian' than a direct historical connection or lineage. It contrasts with and counteracts the idea of cultural citizenship discussed in Chapter 2, as well as Teo's observation (2006) that there were many more ways of being Australian in the previous decade. Discourses of civic nationalism have also been criticized for negating the significance of past wrongdoing (even colonization and slavery) by people who can today be considered 'Real Australians' on the basis of the contribution that they make – regardless of their political associations or the past atrocities of their ancestors – to the nation. In this formulation, 'nationalism' becomes part of a positive and progressive multicultural mythology that overwrites 'race' (Lentin and Bensaidi 2015; Frances 2016; Tan 2017).[10] 'Instead of national identity defined along the lines of a primarily cultural (here: white) heritage', explains Frances (2016), it 'offers a tale of a shared investment in the "Australian" state'.

The shift towards a mainstream adoption of civic nationalism reflects a changing field of contemporary political discourse. The changes were acute in the 1990s, as a decade in which far right-wing politician Pauline Hanson and her One Nation party came to prominence.[11] At this time, according to Howard, Australia was a country searching for a more 'comfortable' past, and as unlikely as it might sound, the narrative of migration offered a less-problematic alternative to both xenophobic white Australian political voices and so-called black armband histories.[12] Howard expressed the desire for Australians to feel 'comfortable and relaxed' about their history (Attwood 2005: 33–4). Although the perspective of the 'Real Australians' poster campaign is ideologically divergent from that represented by Howard, both employ an image of civic nationalism. 'Australians', represented as heterogeneous by Drew and homogenous by Howard, are encouraged to subscribe to a myth of Australian-ness that sweeps racist legacies 'under the rug by projections of acceptance back into the past' by recognizing the contribution to Australian society of members of long-gone generations of migrants such as Monga Khan who had been previously maligned by public opinion or subject to racist government policies such as the White Australia Policy (Frances 2016).

It is likely that Drew's posters unintentionally reflected and perhaps took on board some of the characteristics of the changes in political discourse occurring in recent years, even as he attempted to critique these. Whatever the reason, however, the posters have been criticized for (*i*) displacing race in favour of a counter-discourse of civic multiculturalism or civic nationalism (where being Australian results from actions not skin colour), and (*ii*) white-washing colonial injustice, genocide and the need for contemporary responsibility to be taken over the legacies of these actions. These arguments have developed from observations that Drew's posters perform the authority to accept (that is welcome or else request welcome on behalf of) non-white identities that are presumed to require the assistance of such forms of governance to be accorded national identity. This effect is heightened by the location of posters within the 'middle ground' of shared urban areas which are associated with the generic national imaginary of the public sphere and double as spaces of social management (Bennett 2015). In reiterating a need for acceptance of racial differences (the non-white body) within a contemporary inclusive multicultural civic space (that is primarily middle-class and white), Drew's posters rely on the same racial distinctions that the version of nationalism they promote seeks to denounce.

Structural racism[13]

Scholars and theorists of language, culture, and politics have also engaged critically with the lexicon represented by Drew's posters. The perception that white Australians have the authority to confer the title 'Real Aussie' upon non-white identities accords with Ghassan Hage's analysis in *White Nation*, an examination of responses by white Australians to multiculturalism (Hage 1988).[14] Hage, an anthropologist and social theorist, argues that there is a similarity in positioning between anti-racist 'multiculturalists' who support cultural and ethnic diversity and anti-anti-racists (such as Pauline Hanson or conservative media commentator, Andrew Bolt) who do not. Both positions, he argues, claim a normalized middle ground and both speak from this shared position of privilege and the entitlement to govern or socially manage difference. Regardless of having different messages, they both occupy a position of power that is required for them to have the authority to speak. Hage argues that this position is not 'naturally' attributed to non-white identities. In this view of multiculturalism, the white Australian majority enjoy 'having' diversity in their lives. Migrants and asylum seekers are perceived to add diversity (through the depoliticized stereotype of 'food, festivals, folklore and fashion'), but their cultures are something that can be authorized or not, and their access to basic services can be managed by the dominant (white) Australian cultural cohort. In other words, 'good white nationalists' (Hage 1988: 78–104) continue to enjoy and exercise arbitration over who has the right to welcome whom.

Hage's position has been extended by race theorist Alana Lentin, who argues that liberal democratic culture (which typically gives rise to civic nationalism) establishes the structures and policies – including multiculturalism – that normalize the conditions through which racism appears to counter the dominant image of an intrinsically non-racist Australian multicultural centre. The common-sense middle ground is generally recognized as being the space of an Australian 'fair go' nationalism, which is set in opposition to any extreme views or behaviours. This normalized middle ground and its associated basis in a presumed/fabricated 'common-sense' evidences the impact that Howard's preference for 'comfortable history' has had on the national imaginary across the last twenty years. Although not representative of an overt form of racism such as that proclaimed by xenophobic organizations like Reclaim Australia, or the insidious form of anti-anti-racism (I'm not racist, but . . .'), the 'Real Australians' campaign can be seen to evidence, and may be a symptom of, structural racism on the grounds that it maintains the right of the centre to gift welcome (attribute nationhood) at the same time as it maintains the incongruous fantasy (Hage 1988) of being an accepting and inclusive champion of a progressive multicultural society.[15] In a critique that could apply to the 'Real Australians Say Welcome' campaign, Lentin and Bensaidi (2015) say, 'The fact that an anti-racist initiative uses the language of nationalist authenticity – "real Australians" – is revealing of the fact that organizations like Welcome to Australia mainly talk among themselves; the supposed "ordinary" (read: white) Australians'.

This debate has clear implications for museums that seek to engage with questions of national identity. Chapter 2, for example, explored the paradoxical situation the National Museum of Australia found itself in upon opening, where it was derided as 'too political' and as 'un museum-like' by conservative Australian politicians and commentators, despite the orientation of its founding document that the museum, 'where appropriate, should display controversial issues . . . too many museums concentrate on certainty and dogma, thereby forsaking the function of stimulating legitimate doubt and thoughtful discussion' (Commonwealth Government 1975: 73; also see Anderson 2011). While the Immigration Museum by and large avoided getting tied up in the political and public contestation surrounding the opening of the National Museum of Australia, it has not entirely escaped criticism from museum professionals and scholars. Hage criticized the museum on similar grounds to those levelled subsequently by others against Drew's work, for its perpetration of the conditions of structural racism that it *prima facie* seeks to challenge (McFadzean 2017).[16] In claiming that the museum ostensibly occupies the problematic middle ground of white privilege and authority (that Drew's posters have been critiqued as reaffirming), Hage's argument builds both on social theory and on the significant body of historical research showing museums as colonial and contemporary instruments of governance and social management (see Chapter 1), whereby they fundamentally exist as a condition of structural racism – a condition that has been addressed in museum theory as the social management of cultural difference (Bennett 2015).

Hage's criticism engages with the institutional and political framework within which museums operate, and certainly needs to be accommodated within the exhibition and program work undertaken by museums – a point curatorial staff generally agree with strongly.[17] However, the response by curator Moya McFadzeon to Hage is also valuable, not the least for its articulation of the potential contribution that museums *can* uniquely make – not just to the 'management' of race hate speech (Shoshan 2016: 6), but in relation to providing a platform for the experience of such. McFadzean (2017) recalls her interaction with Hage as having played out in the following way:

> It was quite confronting . . . I felt like saying, 'It's only favorable for you. You just write your books and you send them out there and that's great'. I love what he [Hage] writes, mind you. Don't get me wrong but we can't do that at an Immigration Museum. There are pragmatics about being a museum and it's about relationships and communities. It's got to be about validation and celebration, as well as, reality and the dark stuff too. . . . I was trying to say, 'We walk the difficult tightrope in terms of interpretation, in terms about being a space for people to have their festivals and celebrate their cultures and bring people together and talk about racism, and talk about the history of immigration'. I think what I'm getting to is I think it's becoming more and more complicated, not less so.

Regardless of Hage's critique, and despite the complexity of the political and social field within which the museum opened in 1998 (McFadzean 2017), just three years earlier than the National Museum of Australia, it attracted very little public backlash or negative political interest at its launch (Stone 1998). This contrast might be because a museum of immigration was more likely to be seen at that time as being a museum about and for 'others'. Perceived as being in the mould, for example, of Australia's only other similar museum (the Migration Museum, in South Australia, which had opened in 1986), it was likely considered a museum for ethnic communities to represent themselves, in contrast with the National Museum of Australia, which was held to account on the grounds that it should represent the authentic heritage of 'Real Australians'. This interpretation extends the false association of multiculturalism with migration (discussed in Chapter 1), and the connected view that where 'Real Australians' are defined through their political identity (Australian citizenship), migrants, 'new Australians' and any other 'would be Australians' (including asylum seekers) are defined instead as having a predominantly 'cultural' identity.[18] As well as reflecting the context of structural racism into which the museum opened, this response failed to acknowledge the statements made by the Immigration Museum at its opening about its mission and remit, which explicitly represented the museum as a politicized space of cultural diversity that would represent and reflect 'all Australians' through its invocation for all visitors to come in and 'find your own story'. The museum's agenda was described by Richard Gillespie as seeking to engage with debates over 'immigration', which:

> has regularly been a hotly contested political issue – over intake levels, "appropriate" countries of origin, and policies of exclusion, assimilation or multiculturalism – it has also been a theme that links family and personal experiences to the larger shifts and patterns in Australia's history.
>
> (Gillespie 2001: 263)

The museum's intention to contribute to and assert agency within a political sphere (rather than just being a space of culture for migrants) was indicated at its opening by statements made by museum staff and by the exhibitions themselves, including within the *Impacts* gallery (1998–2002) that included 'stop the racists' badges and controversies about Australia's immigration policies, the White Australia policy, and multiculturalism. Although the museum did find itself the target of hostility in 2011 from some extremists with the opening of *Identity: yours, mine, ours* (as discussed shortly), previous exhibitions did not attract substantive negative public attention, even *Getting In: Australia's Immigration Policies, Past and Present*, an exhibition that opened in 2003 and encouraged visitors to explore and experience the processes of entry that migrants to Australia undergo and the bureaucratic policy structures around Australian immigration policy (see Chapter 1). McFadzeon's description about the museum's approach is, like Gillespie's, unambiguous:

> The [museum's] principal themes are innately confronting and have the potential to be controversial. For example, nation-building may be explored in terms of the philosophies and strategies of Australian immigration policy which have always revolved around questions of national identity – what sort of nation do we want to establish? What kind of people do we want living here and being 'Australians'? What can people offer us that will be of use? These questions were being asked at the time of Federation and are being asked today.
>
> (McFadzeon 2002)

My assessment is that ultimately, and regardless of the National Museum's enthusiasm for playing into the culture wars (Casey quoted in Chapter 2), the Immigration Museum did not face the same level of hostility from the public and some politicians because the National Museum of Australia was seen as a remnant of an earlier political regime and ideology that the current national government did not adhere to or support (Anderson 2011). In contrast, the Immigration Museum opened with the full backing of the Victorian Government. McFadzean (2017) also suggests this point regarding *Getting In: Australia's Immigration Policies, Past and Present*, about which she said: 'I swear we couldn't have done that exhibition at that time with that government at the NMA [National Museum of Australia]. There's no way'.

Government policy is not widely understood

More than just enjoying government support for the contribution it was trying to make to encourage a firm sense of public and community 'ownership' of the immigration story (The Immigration Museum Consultancy Group 1994, Part 1: Introduction, p. 1), the museum had been tasked from the outset with representing multicultural policy. This was recognized as important because multicultural policy had been reported as having been poorly understood by Australians over many decades. A study by Carol Bailey compared research conducted by Mackay a decade apart (1985 and 1995) into Australians' attitudes towards multiculturalism:

> Both reports demonstrate that there is considerable confusion, bewilderment and ignorance surrounding government policy on MC [multiculturalism] and immigration, leading to prejudice and speculation. The same sorts of questions which appeared in 1985 ('What is the government policy on immigration anyway?') reappear in 1995. People are confused about whether or not there is a definite policy; whether certain groups are encouraged; how the points system works; whether there is a skills requirement, and if so which skills are wanted; who is allowed in under the family reunion scheme; what quotas operate; where refugees fit in and so on.
>
> (Bailey 1995)

Mackay's 1995 paper concluded by stating that wider public debate is needed to address the 'very real concerns of many Australians and calls for a public forum to more fully discuss the desired outcomes of multicultural and immigration policy and the future directions for Australian society'.[19] Such a forum must encourage civil discourse, and be 'free from both the excesses of hate speech and the strictures of political correctness' (Bailey 1995: 1). Bailey's observations, particularly around the need for a 'forum' were reiterated both in the museum's development planning process undertaken by external consultants[20] as well as in reflections made in 1997 (just a year prior to the opening of the museum) by another report commissioned by the Australian Government, which similarly observed that immigration and multiculturalism:

> continue to be major issues for Australians concerned about the state of the nation and its future. Debate on these topics is however often heated and not well informed . . . not because they are necessarily unpopular, but because they are widely misunderstood, and lack a clear rationale.
>
> (Holton 1997)

That the museum was designed with the intention to contribute to efforts geared toward improving general levels of policy knowledge amongst Australians is confirmed in its planning documents, one of which presents the museum's potential as being 'to assist the Government of Victoria in its commitment to Ethnic Affairs by promoting a deeper understanding and appreciation of Australia's ethnic heritage' (The Immigration Museum Consultancy Group 1994, Introduction (Background to study): 1–2).

It is interesting to compare these reports with research undertaken in the process of consulting about the development of the Immigration Museum in the lead up to the Kennett government's support of the Station Pier proposal. The language (and findings) employed in the final report and Station Pier proposal are very similar to what is described by Bailey (1995) and Holton (1997), and strongly reiterates the language employed by Howard and an underlying condition of structural racism. The Station Pier proposal said: 'In the 1990s, Australia has matured into a rich cultural matrix that is both interesting and unique, and, which, in overall terms, has tolerance of diversity as a core value' (The Immigration Museum Consultancy Group 1994, Part 1: 1–6; also Zubrzycki 1995). In the fundraising and marketing section (which recommends developing a donor program 'to tap into all those Australians who have dispersed around the country from the historic arrival point' (The Immigration Museum Consultancy Group 1994, Part 6: 6–7), it states 'Victorians, Australians and tourists will see the Museum as a monument to all those who have started new lives here, publicly validating their contributions to society' (The Immigration Museum Consultancy Group 1994, Part 6: 6–2).

The proposal's language of 'tolerance' and 'validation of contributions' reiterates the idea that being a 'good', civic minded Australian will diminish cultural differences (such that similarities should be emphasized as what unifies the nation; rather than the differences between people who embody the imaginary space). Illustrating the continuing provisional nature of being granted 'welcome' and citizenship in Australia, the proposal says: 'The policy of multiculturalism gave ethnic minorities official permission to challenge previous understandings that their task was to assimilate. Instead, it released them, and by implication, all Australians, to reflect on new and broader understandings of what is constituted as "Australian"' (The Immigration Museum Consultancy Group 1994, Part 3: The Museum: 3–2). The language of 'permission' extends throughout the final conclusions offered by the consultants (see also The Immigration Museum Consultancy Group 1994, Part 3: The Museum: 3–3).

More warning than welcome[21]

Whilst Immigration Museum programs and exhibitions (including *Getting In: Australia's Immigration Policies, Past and Present*) have sought to challenge the institution's associations with the views of civic nationalism represented in some of its planning documents, the public sphere in which the museum exists has continued to be marked by the categories of 'Real Australian' and 'un-Australian'. These concepts have also continued to feature in the Australian political landscape, as illustrated by the Australian Government's release in 2017 of a new statement (released on March 21, 'Harmony Day') redefining what it means to be part of 'multicultural Australia' (Australian Government 2017). The new statement uses language consistent with Drew's campaigns, and the broader invocation to a context of multicultural nationalism that highlights the obligations associated with being acknowledged ('welcomed') as a 'Real Australian'. According to the new statement: 'Today, Australians welcome those who have migrated here to be part of our free and open society, to build their lives and make a contribution to our nation' (Australian Government 2017: 7). Australian Senator and leader of the Australian Greens Party, Richard Di Natale, jumped on the new statement immediately, cautioning that it was 'more warning than welcome' to prospective real Australians (Di Natale 2017).

The new statement does not appear to be substantively different from the previous version (released by a Labor government under Prime Minister Julia Gillard in 1996 and updated in 2011 under the title 'The People of Australia') in terms of the language and rhetorical tools employed. However, even while no accompanying 'policy' was released to guide the new statement's implementation, it does register some differences from the previous Gillard policy, namely over the emphasis accorded to global terrorism threats, the integration and national security over social inclusion and equality, some divergent language (for example, replacing 'equality of outcome' with 'equality of opportunity'), and a redrawing of language and obligations associated with 'Australian values' and citizenship (such that 'race' re-appears in the national lexicon and the phrase 'equity' is removed).

Despite not shepherding the establishment of a new multicultural statement under his leadership until 2017, Prime Minister Malcolm Turnbull (who took office in 2015) has typically addressed multiculturalism as a key corrective for extremism and a signal of Australia's progressive cos-mopolitanism (a point enthusiastically also explored by museums such as the National Museum of Australia, see Chapter 2, also Ang 2009). Indeed, he has even argued that multiculturalism is the country's great-est asset – a key characteristic of the ' "fundamental Australian value" of mutual respect' (quoted in Hurst and Medhora 2015). Multiculturalism in this view is not, *prima facie*, something to attribute to ethnic 'others' who do not 'assimilate' to Australian norms, and neither is it a more likely con-dition for terrorism or un-Australian behaviours (as per the stated belief of his predecessor, Prime Minister Tony Abbott),[22] but is a signifier of a sophisticated and inclusive middle ground; a space occupied by Austral-ians of diverse cultural backgrounds who are generous and tolerant enough to offer 'welcome' to those likely to make a contribution to the nation. In this formulation, the middle ground of civic – multicultural – nationalism (that employs the parameters of the 'white nation' described by Hage 1988) sits in opposition to a range of violent extremisms, from anti-Australian/ Western terrorism to 'those people who decide that the response to the extremism of a very small minority is to vilify all Muslims. . . . That is the most counterproductive thing you can do' (Turnbull quoted in Hurst and Medhora 2015).

Turnbull's rhetoric, even at the same time as it congratulates the inclusiv-ity and fundamental 'reasonableness' of the Australian nation, problemati-cally allows for a greater range and diversity of threats than Abbott's more simplistic 'them versus us' model. By focusing on the obligations rather the rights of citizenship it also further emphasizes the conditionality of this welcome. Whereas Abbott's term, 'Team Australia', was coined to engen-der a tough stand against external terrorist threats (including 'queue jumper' asylum seekers as per his 'return the boats' campaign (Abbott 2013; Kelly 2012), the 'Real (multicultural) Australians' framework creates the condi-tions for a broader range of would-be Australians that double as poten-tial threats, which also includes those ('home-grown' threats) amongst us (Hurst and Medhora 2015). Di Natale's comment that the new statement is 'more warning than welcome' recognizes the Australian Government's shift to identify an enlarged pool of potential threats (of which the new statement is part).[23] His comment his statement combines with Turnbull's, to show the point made by Hage (1988), Bennett (2015) and others, that multiculturalism continues to exist as an enduring and important tool of social (and self) management that tolerates a broader field of everyday rac-ism under the guise of people 'getting along' but that ultimately reasserts the 'naturalness' of a white nation that tolerates the non-white body as long as it suits.[24] It also demonstrates the importance of language and of shifts in public discourse over time.

Politics is not about other people, museums are not about other people

> While political elites have become particularly adept at avoiding the use of the category 'race', supplanting it with de-racialized terms such as 'culture', there are nonetheless occasions when 'race' is worth the risk in allowing a political speaker to conjure fear inducing imagery and causal inference in ways that advance a political project.
>
> (Augoustinos and Every 2010: 254)

In the years since it opened, the Immigration Museum has taken on an increasingly confident political role, perhaps buoyed as a result of avoiding the culture wars debate that ensconced the National Museum of Australia, but also out of a commitment to demonstrating the processes, and perhaps costs, involved in risk-taking.[25] *Identity: yours, mine, ours*, a permanent exhibition which opened at the Immigration Museum in Melbourne on May 9 2011, has represented their clearest engagement in political and public debates thus far – a conscious decision that was explained in planning documents as being because it was 'time for IM to move into subject matter beyond immediate migrant experience and into broader social histories, issues and impacts of migration', including topics that are 'timely, relevant, challenging, extremely important', which would mean developing a more contemporary focus and 'expanding our role as an important focal point for discussing contemporary issues and supporting social change' (Immigration Museum 2009a). Working project aims that informed the exhibition's development included:

- To position the Immigration Museum as a key site for counteracting racism and promoting social cohesion [indeed, an earlier document included as an aim 'To position the Immigration Museum in a leadership role by taking a stand against racism' (Immigration Museum 2008)].
- To create a historic context for notions of race and identity, to help visitors better understand their own and others' attitudes.
- To provide an uplifting, informative exhibition that nonetheless addresses difficult social issues.
- To be a forum for educating about cultural sensitivities.
- To create a fearless and sometimes confronting exhibition which provides community discussion and supports positive social change, and contributes to personal learning.

(Immigration Museum 2009b).

One representative story in the exhibition is told by Nguyen Hong Duc, one of 200 children airlifted from Vietnam to Australia during 'Operation

Babylift' in 1975 (shortly before Hieu Van Le's arrival by boat in Australia). Renamed Dominic, he was raised on a farm in South Australia by the Golding family. Reflecting an acknowledgment that 'identity is hard to reflect through material culture' (Immigration Museum 2009e), as well as the museum's ongoing interest in utilizing the material culture of government policy and administrative processes (Immigration Museum 2009b) – which had, it was noted, continued to be poorly understood in the period following Bailey's analysis (Bailey 1995; Immigration Museum 2008) – the exhibition displays an entry permit belonging to Dominic, who says:

> I was a four month old orphan when I was given this permit in 1975. Bundled up, I was handed to strangers in Melbourne. This new family gave me a new home, name and a better future. But I'll never find my first mother and father. It's as though the passport erased a family to create a family.

This is one of the many stories included in the exhibition that focuses on how cultural heritage, languages, beliefs, and family connections influence self-perceptions and the images we have of other people – as impressions that can, the exhibition text advises, lead to 'discovery, confusion, prejudice and understanding'. Exemplifying the exhibition's aim 'to provide an uplifting, informative exhibition that nonetheless addresses difficult social issues', *Identity: yours, mine, ours* is constituted by stories such as Dominic's, which are about identity, culture, race, and the way people communicate to maintain or challenge the categories and experiences that sit behind these terms. This display also illustrates a central communication strategy employed throughout the exhibition, which is to present notions of identity (ethnicity, religion, and language) in relation to multiple identities, ongoing discussion and interpretations of Australian identity (including definitions and roles of citizenship in creating identities), and concepts of race, racism, and prejudice by placing the exhibition's emphasis on 'making these concepts real and human through personal experiences' (Immigration Museum 2009a).

Consistent with Bangstad's recommendation (2017, outlined in Chapter 1), this approach was designed to centralize an interpretive experience in which the experience of racism was represented in the voice of Australians to extend the exhibition's 'key priority', which was, above all, to be relevant. Planning documents explained that this would mean that the exhibition should:

- Be significant (cognitive)
    - Socially and culturally significant information, real and not trivial – 'this is important information to know!'

- A sense of ownership over content – 'I cant believe this!' [This statement leverages the museum's earlier aims for community ownership over the museum as a site of otherness – note that it is now speaking from a position of authority.]
- Information that connects to own experience – 'This has relevance to me!' (Immigration Museum 2009c: 6).

The exhibition is divided conceptually into three broad sections: 'First impressions', 'People like us', and 'People like them'. Its main narrative framework is structured around the pairing of ideas about identity and belonging. The exhibition shows that identity is typically understood as being associated with individuals and personal subjectivity, while belonging is often perceived as arising from and being about community. However, it also asks visitors to consider these terms as not being bound by rigid dichotomies or definitions, but to focus instead on the relationships between them. The emphasis on relationality is made explicit by including the museum as an actor within the network of relationships, and curators were well aware of how:

> Important [it is] to explore how hard and real the stories can be (IM often gets comments that we "only explore the happy stories") EG: "why are young males negative to new migrants?" Would be interesting to see what would be their questions about experiences of race and identity.
>
> (Immigration Museum 2009d)

Focusing attention on the 'spectrum' of processes by which identity, identification, and belonging are formed or damaged by interpersonal, cultural, and institutional norms and relationships, the exhibition asks visitors to consider ways in which (individual) identity and belonging (to community or nation) both complement and undercut each other. In addition to providing a context for the exhibition, this framework also effectively constitutes the 'terms of engagement' or 'ground rules' that visitors will adopt when they enter the space: not only will visitors engage from the heart and with integrity and self-reflection, but they will be challenged to articulate and examine their own responses, perceptions, and prejudices.

The expectation that visitors will respond empathetically to the exhibition is made clear throughout the exhibition but is perhaps most acute in the opening display. Visitors are met by a human scaled video artwork by Lynette Wallworth that presents a series of different groups some are family groupings, while others are identifiable as schoolmates, or as belonging to some other community or interest group. Some groups welcome visitors openly, while others stand aggressively or defensively in their pose and facial expressions. Wallworth explains that the video work was intended to reflect the nuances of social inclusion or exclusion and associated feelings of belonging or alienation: 'We have the means via the smallest gesture to include or exclude and to signal whether someone is an outsider or not. We defend invisible territories or we give ground, and all without a word being uttered'. Visitors are passive in the face of this orientation video. The only options available to them are to react and reflect silently, to express their feelings to fellow exhibition visitors, or leave the exhibition: there is no point in talking back to a video wall. As visitors pass this display and progress through the exhibition, however, they are encouraged, then invited, and then finally, expected to articulate their perceptions and positions on certain issues. A transition occurs through a process of education whereby visitors start by being subjected and voiceless in the first display to gaining agency and the authority to communicate their views. In the final part of the exhibition, visitors are explicitly tasked with the responsibility of putting into words their reactions.

The exhibition's central concerns are with social action as well as the processes of relationship building, breakdown, and mending, and it conveys the critical message that efforts to combat racism require a multifaceted process that is increasingly intertwined with efforts to address the tensions of diversity. My main reason for focusing on *Identity: yours, mine, ours* is to explore the context, intent, processes, and outcomes of the curatorial decision to reintroduce racism to public debate, which was done quite deliberately, and through an extensive process of consultation to represent Australians' perceptions and experiences of racism, and if and how it has acted 'to combat racism and its pernicious effects today' (Golding 2009: 2. Consultation included, for example, Immigration Museum 2009f; Museum Victoria 2009; Immigration Museum 2010a).[26]

My analysis of the exhibition employs an 'anti-racist praxis' that positions the exhibition within and reflects upon a wider field of media texts and public debate that has, in recent years, done much to disguise and normalize racism within a nationalist discourse. In the final instance, I argue that the exhibition exists as a political project, and that an 'anti-racist' praxis influenced and permeates all elements of the design and content of *Identity: yours, mine, ours*. Racism was a motivating theme for the exhibition from its earliest planning days (which had the working title 'Identity and Race in Australia') (Immigration Museum 2008), and the curators and others involved in the project's development had the clear aim of focusing on 'the visitor and visitor attitudes, and its main outcome will be to make a difference in our society' (Immigration Museum 2009b). There was also broad recognition, however, of the challenges associated with meeting this goal (Immigration Museum 2009b).[27]

Defining racism

> In my experience there can be a perception amongst people that racism is a binary – you are racist, or you are not racist – and that people who are racist are really racist and hold attitudes like apartheid South Africa. In reality, racism is more of a spectrum. . . . We live in a society that is racist (or to put it another way, which privileges some races over others) and it is practically impossible not to pick up some racist thinking as a result.
>
> (Anonymous response to online survey, Australian
> Human Rights Commission 2012: 21)

This section has two starting points. The first is an acknowledgment that museums can provide an opportunity to talk across 'race lines' (Australian Human Rights Commission 2012: 13). The second is the word 'racism'. *Identity: yours, mine, ours* shows that the possibility of talking across boundaries or differences exists in museums located at the intersection of the public/community sector, the public policy/government sector, and the education sector (schools and universities), as well as other spheres, including the media, community, and corporate sectors (for a sample range of stakeholder consultations undertaken in the development of the exhibition, see Immigration Museum 2009f; Museum Victoria 2009; Immigration Museum 2010a). The exhibition also demonstrates the point that exhibitions or museums that aim to engage audiences in critical thinking about stereotypes in society, or which seek to produce critical engagement with key contemporary issues around race, migration, colonization, and multiculturalism highlight, amongst other things, different understandings, and definitions that various sectors have of different terminology and concepts. Central amongst these is racism, which is defined by academic researchers, Gabrielle Berman and Yin Paradies (2008: 228), as 'that which maintains or exacerbates inequality of opportunities among ethnoracial groups'. Racism can, these authors suggest, 'be expressed through stereotypes (racist beliefs), prejudice (racist emotions/affect) or discrimination (racist behaviors and practices)'. While academic definitions of racism are likely to emphasize prejudice, power, ideology, stereotypes, domination, disparities, and/or unequal treatment, alternative perceptions or understandings about the term 'racism' can be seen in textual analysis of media reports of race or ethnic or class based clashes globally. It was also a term that was identified as divisive by participants in the extensive process of consultation that was undertaken as part of the exhibition's development,[28] and which contributed to 'race' being removed from the exhibition title.

As this book has already argued, migration museums engage with questions and challenges around rights in ways that have tended to reflect public policy phases. This is also evident in *Identity: yours, mine, ours*, which was created as an educational tool aligned with the Australian Human Rights Commission's attempt to fight racism by naming it and putting it on the national agenda (McFadzean 2012; Szoke 2012). While I outlined earlier policy approaches in previous chapters, policies of the mid-late 2000s – the period in which this exhibition was developed – were influenced by a pervasive 'cultural turn' that spread across academic thinking at this time, and which extended what Alana Lentin (2005; in Berman and Paradies 2008: 220) called a 'shift towards culture as opposed to race, with the outcome being the evolution of a state of "racelessness" '. Aspirational policies based on ideologies of a 'color-blind' or 'raceless' society cannot be entirely problem-free, however, because they 'obviate the anti-racist efforts that are a necessary precondition for securing the rights of all members of a society' (Berman and Paradies 2008: 220). In Australia at this time, the trend was to present all differences as being of equal value, and as constituting no impediment to unity ('everybody can succeed if they try hard enough') (Augoustinos, Le Couteur and Soyland 2002: 109).

Although the ideal of inter-personal 'tolerance' was maintained through this period, government rhetoric, in which the phrase cultural diversity became the preferred terminology to address difference, reflected the attitude that 'actually we are not all the same (which implies there is something wrong with being different), but we are all different' (Bennett 2012). The increasing recognition of difference drew attention to the issues and challenges that needed to be overcome if equity was to be achieved. However confusion over the reach and parameters (if not purpose) of multiculturalism (as an adequate umbrella term for all policy developments since the 1970s) in addressing disadvantage and combating racism contributed to a marginalization of anti-racism measures through this period (Berman and Paradies 2008). While racism was strenuously denied as a motivation for policy-making at this time, proclamations about the 'failure' of multiculturalism featured prominently in government discourses across Europe (notably in the United Kingdom, but also in France and elsewhere).[29] It was in response to this situation that Ien Ang (2009) wrote: 'Beyond multiculturalism: A journey to nowhere?' A backlash period reflecting fears about terrorism and the national debates about asylum seekers (in Australia at least) provided a transition into an era in which 'cultural racism' became the dominant concept and narrative.

The Australian Government's interest in bringing the term 'racism' explicitly back into mainstream public dialogue was signaled in 2007 when it was identified by the recently elected Labor government as an element of their social inclusion strategies (Gillard and Wong 2007; Gillard and Macklin 2009). A high-profile public campaign, 'Racism: It stops with me', was launched in 2012 in association with a new National Anti-Racism strategy by the Australian Human Rights Commission that focused on building close partnerships with individuals and organizations from all parts of the Australian community (Australian Human Rights Commission 2012). The Strategy's three main goals set out to achieve: (a) recognition amongst more Australians that racism continues to be a serious issue in our community; (b) the involvement of more Australians in practical actions to tackle racism, wherever they see it; and (c) increased awareness by individuals about how to access the resources they need to address racism, to access legal protections, and where necessary, to obtain redress. As illustrated by its key question, 'How does racism make you feel?', the Strategy aimed to solicit empathy at an individual level but demands action from 'you' as a socially aware and responsible member of a group (be it a sporting group, school, etc.). The changes emerging in government policy at this time were motivated by recognition that the three dominant and interconnected forms of racism – institutional, interpersonal, and systemic – need to be tackled across government, community, and interpersonal relationships and frameworks. The changes also act on recognition expressed in community consultation that 'tolerance' discourses have become synonymous with punitive processes for dealing with problems of difference/exclusion such as antisocial behaviour and the refusal to participate in norms associated with a common citizenship (Bennett 2012).

The National Anti-Racism Strategy was designed to address the causes as well as the symptoms of racism in Australia, and to build on groundwork provided by the current Australian Government policy, *The People of Australia – Australia's Multicultural Policy* launched in February 2011 (Australian Government 2011). It acknowledged as insufficient previous initiatives that addressed only the symptoms of racism, arguing that this approach can both feed a backlash and continue or extend the structural inequalities endemic within earlier policy phases. The new strategy also responded to a sense that the absence of the word 'racism' from the policy sphere and public debate meant that members of the public have had no reason to understand their behaviour or attitudes as being racist (or not). This suggestion, increasingly made by academics and some policy-makers, has been supported by an escalating trend of 'anti-anti racism' statements apparent in the media and public sphere. Often manifested in 'I'm no racist, but . . .' (Innes 2011) types of comments, and associated with a conviction that an overly engineered political correctness has led to an overzealous anti-racism that has become a significant social problem,[30] this anti-intellectual sentiment is apparent in the extreme responses to *Identity: yours, mine, ours* and the media's reporting of the 'Flags on cars for Australia Day' research. The 'I'm not racist but . . .' statement functions as a persuasive discursive disclaimer intended to distance a speaker from any charge of prejudice and solicit a feeling of agreement (or community) with the listener, whilst also conveying negative views about a minority group. It exists as a form of active disengagement, which might be understood as registering a discomfort on the part of the speaker that may in turn indicate a feeling of being challenged or confused by the exhibition content.

In describing her understanding of the potential that museums have to talk or enable talk across a range of what we might call 'differencing lines' (keeping in mind Tony Bennett's (2005: 14) argument that museums function as 'differencing machines'), Viv Golding (2009: 2) has argued that we need to be attuned to:

> the way in which the meaning of certain pernicious ideas about 'other' peoples and their cultures, which appear to be based on obvious factual evidence can change when they are questioned in between locations, at the frontiers of traditional disciplinary boundaries, and beyond the confines of institutional spaces.

The renewed attention to racism in the public/community sector and public policy/government sector reflects a commitment to this process of looking anew, and has been reflected in attempts by museums to engage in and encourage better frameworks for understanding social justice issues and the battle against racism in any form (including anti-anti racism). The history of the transformation of museum methodologies within the various, increasingly interdisciplinary, theme or identity specific museums that have been developed over the past half-century or so (see Chapter 1) is also implicitly evident in *Identity: yours, mine, ours*, which adopts different modes in different display elements. In its final form, the exhibition also provides an example of the increasing openness and responsiveness of museums to prompts from social science researchers in fields including psychology and sociology, where the emergence of new methodologies for engaging with racism is being extensively reported (Paradies 2012). These historical and contemporary elements combine to generate an attempt to transgress traditional rationales for collecting (where, for example, the material culture of Indigenous peoples was categorized as ethnography and the productions of Western peoples as national history or fine art). The effect is an exhibition that is engaged in contemporary debate, which also presents a reflective approach to understanding the nineteenth-century public museum's pedagogic aims of universal education as well as the ideologies of imperialism and social Darwinism to which museums are intimately connected and from which their collections were made *sensible*.

Reflection on the role of 'the museum' as a governmental apparatus in the normalization of racism has occurred primarily in *Identity: yours, mine, ours* through a process of repositioning collections that has been intended to set up a double gaze whereby objects are used to show both unconstructed national stereotypes and post-national narratives (Mason 2012). This happens in two ways. First, through the physical design of the space, where the confronting tram incident explored in 'Who's Next Door?' is followed with displays about seemingly harmless stereotypes in everyday products and advertising where, to quote the wall-text:

> ' "black" faces sell chocolates, coffee and biscuits. "Oriental" faces sell rice and crackers. Advertising jingles use comical characters and "funny" accents to sell everything from pasta sauce to washing machines' (exhibition text).

Second, material culture that may have been previously categorized as either ethnographic or traditional folklife (for example traditional costumes or dolls)[31] has been placed alongside ephemera and items from contemporary culture (including a black 'hoodie' jacket decorated by Kat Clarke, a young Wotjobaluk woman from western Victoria),[32] or addressed in relation to archival speeches on paper or film (the exhibition presents nationally significant addresses by politicians and then asks visitors to reflect on how these speeches made them feel) to build strong narratives about the lives of people represented in text or video formats.[33]

Approaching racism: methods for analysis

No cut-and-dried definition of racism will be palatable to everyone, however, even a preliminary attempt can be useful for those seeking to understand how racism works in society. Moreover, to move from definitions to understanding we need to identify methods for analysing racism, and despite deploying differing approaches to quantitative and qualitative research methods, social science based policy and cultural studies-type humanities researchers contribute a range of pathways for understanding and better explaining the processes and manifestations of racism. Museum studies researchers, who typically draw research techniques and strategies from both fields *and* often work to diminish the authority of the 'line' that usually separates theory and practice, have, for example, argued for an extended application of their interdisciplinary practices and an integration of structural/institutional and everyday inter- and intra-personal levels of discourse analysis to achieve this goal (Golding 2009). These approaches build on the premise that everyday experiences of racism occur on structural (macro) levels as well as on the micro levels of the street, workplace or playground, and researchers typically endeavour to investigate the ways in which individuals – as actors within a power structure – represent and reproduce racist attitudes through their use of language. 'Individuals' here extend beyond members of the general public to include opinion-makers such as journalists, media commentators, and politicians; a point which also shows the impossibility of drawing any clear distinction or separation between macro and micro levels.

These approaches also recognize that Western societies have typically privileged the rights of the individual over the group, where acts of collective identity (particularly when undertaken by a minority) are often viewed by the dominant majority with suspicion on the basis that group rights conflict with, and have the potential to undermine, the unitary political community (Augoustinos, Le Couteur and Soyland 2002). A unitary political community is achieved by contracting individuals to the state where, in exchange for being socially and morally responsible, individuals are granted rights to political agency that include having the right to vote and stand for office, and access to legal support. The priority given in this system to individuals means that it is not uncommon for arguments and preexisting attitudes over group/community versus individual/personal rights to fuel disputes about citizenship rights and responsibilities, particularly when these concepts are tied to understandings about nationhood. However, animated public engagements with issues or accusations of racism often arise from such disputes. In a regime framed by this set of perceptions, multiculturalism becomes, to quote Ien Ang (2009: 17), 'a divisive ideology that encouraged migrants to maintain their cultural separateness rather than integrating into the Australian mainstream. Its emphasis on difference and diversity flew in the face of the desire for cohesive and unified nationhood'.

The overlap that exists across the actions that occur in macro and micro levels also goes some way to show the extent to which media texts (and museums, as a form of media text) are not only influential or persuasive, but often explicitly directive or purposeful. Teun Van Dijk (1993: 30) explains this process by observing that the major functions of discourse about minorities are persuasive; that is, that 'speakers aim to influence the minds of their listeners or readers in such a way that the opinions or attitudes of the audience either become or remain close(r) to those of the speakers or writer'. Purposive speech may also work to justify or legitimate certain attitudes expressed or actions taken by the speaker or writer. Although discourse analysis approaches have correctly been criticized for their tendency to assume passivity and acquiescence on the part of audiences, conceived as prone subjects, it is also important to recognize that a fuller attention to both micro levels – in relation to everyday racism, for example – can result in richer understandings and analysis of agency across the interpersonal actions and relationships that contribute to any social environment.

Some context for my study of a museum exhibition about racism can be provided by progressing a critical discourse analysis approach in relation to media reports of a contemporaneous study conducted by researchers from the University of Western Australia into the likelihood that people who decorated their cars with Australian national flags for Australia Day were less positive about Australia's ethnic diversity than 'non-flag flyers'.[34] The study showed that the general Australian public – at least those who respond to opinion pieces and participate in talk back radio sessions championed by notably conservative media personalities Alan Jones[35] and Andrew Bolt[36] – exhibited a different understanding of the word 'racist' than the definition used by the academics who conducted the study (Fozdar 2012). Some readers animated by the media's commentary about the research were offended because they understood the term 'racism' to be synonymous with 'Nazism', even though that association had not been made by the research (Fozdar 2012). A contributor to the CrusaderRabbit For Liberty blog made the following observations about the media's coverage of the 'Flags on cars for Australia Day' study:

> Politicians, academics and the left in general want it to be a crime to love your country and it's [sic] traditional values. Human rights and multiculturalism spells the death of the west as we know it. Ever notice how 'nationalism' is often equated with nazism or fascism as well as racism. . . . It's simply another ploy to silence free speech so they can impose their undemocratic version of society on us. Genuine western nationalism is the only guarantor of freedom that we have.
>
> (Kowtow 2012)

Protest about what academics might today call 'cultural' (as opposed to 'biological') racism was also apparent in controversy caused by the *Identity: yours, mine, ours* exhibition. Not long after the exhibition opened, curators discovered that an anti-Muslim blog site, the Australian Islamic Monitor, had identified the exhibition as a site for debate. The exhibition's lead curator, Moya McFadzean, suggested that the museum may have attracted this attention because of pre-launch media coverage relating to one of the exhibition elements about Shanaaz Copeland, a South African-born fashion designer who produces *hijab* in Australian Rules football colours for young Muslim women to wear while playing football or in support of their favorite team. A post on the Australian Islamic Monitor blog, titled 'The day I learned that I am a racist bigot', could have, speculated the writer, been equally appropriately called 'How to instill self-hatred in Australian children' or 'The indoctrination of innocent young minds' or 'I am white, therefore I am a racist'. A subsequent contributor added this comment:

> What a load of dangerous, garbage, anti-white racist (probably the most common form of racism in the world) propaganda this stinking museum is full of. It's devised by some hate-filled jerks to twist

the minds of young western children and try to fill them with the old, 'black armband' view of history and fill them with self loathing. I know I am proud of our western, decent liberal democratic way of life.

(Quoted in McFadzean 2012)

This reaction provides an extreme response to the exhibition's invitation for visitors to engage with broad questions about citizenship, belonging, acceptance, and identity – that is, who we are, who others think we are, and what it means to belong and not belong in Australia. Like Kowtow's remonstration against (the media's characterization of) the 'Flags on cars for Australia Day' study, this reaction to the *Identity: yours, mine, ours* exhibition represents a more extreme opinion than what was generally evident in the 'letters to the editor' type comments and contributions received by mainstream media forums. However, both responses are typical of protests against an 'anti-racist' praxis (Berman and Paradies 2008) that has been heavily employed throughout the exhibition and which is itself sometimes associated with the negative stereotype of 'political correctness gone mad'. The speaker quoted by McFadzean fits Van Dijk's explanation (1992: 90) that:

The person who accuses the other as racist is in turn accused of inverted racism against whites, as oversensitive and exaggerating, as intolerant and generally as 'seeing racism where there is none'. . . . Moreover, such accusations are seen to impose taboos, prevent free speech and a 'true' or 'honest' assessment of the ethnic situation. In other words, denials of racism often turn counter-accusations of intolerant and intolerable anti-racism.

'I'm not racist, but . . .': understanding anti-anti racism

An 'anti-anti' racist discourse is a common feature of the structural racism discussed earlier in this chapter. It enables speakers to actively position themselves as part of a common-sense majority ('I know I am proud of our Western, decent liberal democratic way of life') to suggest that it is not they, but politically correct ideologues, who are the problem. Not only are anti-racist critics depicted as being out of touch with the majority, but they are represented as people who discriminate against a majority white population and undermine the liberal principles of free speech. Although clichéd, statements such as 'everybody should be treated equally', 'minority opinion should not carry more weight than majority opinion', and 'everybody can succeed if they try hard enough' (Augoustinos, Le Couteur and Soyland 2002: 109) are likely to be features of 'anti-anti' racist public discourse.

Researchers have identified these phrases as frequent examples of modern or covert racism that work to close down critical engagement and reflection (Van Dijk 1992; Augoustinos, Le Couteur and Soyland 2002; Augoustinos and Every 2010) on the grounds that they typically appear as so much common-sense that they cannot be questioned. The strategy of appealing to the 'common sense majority' is, for example, apparent in Kowtow's claim that 'Politicians, academics and the left in general want it to be a crime to love your country', a statement which works on the assumption that no rational thinking person would argue against the values of national pride, free speech, and democracy. Here, the 'moral majority' becomes the arbiter of tolerance toward cultural difference, which is accepted so long as that difference does not exceed the dominant group's tolerance. Covert, or indirect, racism is also generated by expressions that appear to say something about a speaker, but which actually present a negative view about the person or group being spoken about. The blame is typically laid with the other person or group because they have made the speaker feel uncomfortable in some way.

Identity: yours, mine, ours challenges the validity of moral majority discourse as employed by broadcasters like Jones and Bolt, and (possibly at its peril) returns the term 'racism' to public discourse in order to engage critically with Augoustinos and Every's observation – apparent also in Kowtow's statement – that 'the category of nation is increasingly taking over from race in legitimating oppressive practices toward minority groups and, indeed, as a means by which to sanitize and deracialize racist discourses' (Augoustinos and Every 2007: 133). The exhibition's invitation for visitors to share their own stories, affirm their own identities and defend their experiences of diversity and racism in our community occurs through the extended reach of the museum's online and community based programs and resources. Attention to community feedback was identified as critical to the exhibition curators' commitment to attempts to 'promote creative and positive attitudinal change' about the difficult topic of racism (McFadzean 2012). Perhaps unsurprisingly, this aim appears to have been met – at least if the comments made by visitors in the museum and online are to be considered exclusively. Comments submitted to the 'Taking a stand' postcards, which asked visitors to complete the sentence 'I confront prejudice by . . .' included: '. . . by asking people, what makes you say that, when they make prejudiced statements' (Sam Perkins, age 16, Geelong); '. . . by talking about equal opportunity law, and letting people know racist jokes are not funny (Cilla, age 35, Melbourne); '. . . by our grandchildren are part ghanian and aussie. Great' (Helen Sandy, age 70, Templestowe); '. . . by remembering to challenge and question my own assumptions and actions' (Zoe, age 24).[37]

TripAdvisor, a website that allows tourists to post reviews, provides a broader set of responses to the exhibition and museum in general.[38] Categorized according to reviewers' assessments (poor, average, very good, excellent), analysis of the reviews clearly shows that negative assessments were articulated in language that focused on how the exhibition made the visitor *feel*, whereas positive reviews were more likely to make less emotive and more politically engaged comments. For example, responses categorized under 'poor' or 'average' include (my emphasis):

- '*Mixed feelings* about this place'. (Reviewed May 11, 2012 by mx52nho, age 35–49 year old man from Liverpool, United Kingdom.)
- '*I do not feel good* with the exhibition on the first floor, which is 'Identity: yours, mine and ours'. The short video *made me feel* all immigrants come to Australia because their own countries are full of disasters, and Australia is the only peace land in the earth. *This made me feel bad* and it's not true'. (Reviewed March 7, 2011 by Ryu0208, an 18–24-year-old woman from Melbourne, Australia.)
- 'The video with the stories of the immigrants although it is well made and moving, *when you re-think about it, it makes you feel frustrated*'. (Reviewed August 18, 2012 by elinaDxxx, a 25–34-year-old woman from Melbourne, Australia.)
- '*I left sad*'. (Reviewed January 2, 2012 by Aliciacch, a woman from Perth, Australia.)

Responses categorized under 'excellent' or 'very good' include:

- 'Informative and fair treatment of a difficult topic'. (Reviewed May 18, 2012 by underock, a 25–34-year-old man from Seattle, Washington.)
- 'It makes you think . . .' (Reviewed April 28, 2012 by copey, a 50–64-year-old man from Edinburgh.)
- 'Museum of Shame'. (Reviewed April 11, 2012 by Ted J, a 65+ year old man from Perth, Australia.)
- 'Pauline Hanson and her fans should have a look at this place to get an idea of why people risk their lives to come to Australia'. (Reviewed January 29, 2012 by Brissy girl, Brisbane, Australia.)
- 'There is a section on level 2 that gets you thinking about yourself as an Aussie and the direction society is taking today'. (Reviewed September 17, 2012 by markcwhistler, Melbourne, Australia.)

The exhibition is most didactic in a display called 'Who's Next Door?', a confronting multimedia program that asks visitors to experience a racist incident, that occurs on public transport, through the eyes of everyone involved. 'How would you react?' asks the wall-text. In the small space of the interactive tram environment, museum visitors are transformed into witnesses of a social injustice and are asked to be accountable for their reactions to the racist incident. The exhibition's social justice agenda is also clearly expressed in the text panel that explains: 'When you take action, you can influence the behaviors of others and feel better about yourself. You can also contribute to making prejudice unacceptable. Silence can be interpreted as approval'. 'Who's Next Door?' exemplifies the exhibition's ideological commitment to promoting equality of opportunity for ethnoracial groups in accord with its aim to demonstrate an anti-racist agenda of equity (Berman and Paradies 2008). It also shows the exhibition designers commitment to elicit purposive engagement from their visitors, a point that featured heavily in conversations held in the lead up the exhibition and which can be illustrated by one astute comment minuted from a team meeting: 'Interpretive methods need discussion: purpose? We are initiating the conversation – how do they [visitors] empower themselves following this?' (Immigration Museum 2009d).

The deliberately purposeful educational mandate of this display (which advises audiences how to behave in certain situations) is mediated – and possibly even counteracted – by elements of the display that remind visitors about the museum's own role, function and authority as a location or site that can enable the articulation of views across various 'lines'. Multivocality occurs in the display, for example, because the interactive exhibit gives equal attention to the thoughts of each of the commuters on the tram who are participating in the racist incident. In addition to representing the differing attitudes of individuals, the display illustrates the museum's ability to speak across macro/structural and micro/everyday and interpersonal 'lines'. In so doing, it effectively represents the 'everyday racism' that Philomena Essed (1991: 2) defines as being that which 'connects structural forces of racism with routine situations in everyday life' and 'links ideological dimensions of racism with daily attitudes of it in everyday life'. The impact of this display is indicated by a comment left by a visitor that 'I confront prejudice by using public transport' (Kj, age 43, Melbourne).

The attempt to encourage individual reflection is extended though questions about what it means to define, belong, or be excluded from a broader national polity as well as minority or other specialized groups. 'How does racism affect the community?' is asked at various points of the exhibition to emphasize the cost of racism both for individuals and to broader projects of community-building, and it shows its prevalence and impact in everyday life. The concern reflects comments in the National Anti-Racism Strategy's (Australian Human Rights Commission 2012: 11) report about its consultation process: 'There was a common view shared that being part of a team can be the "glue that holds us together"'. However, the exhibition does more than illustrate the cultural capital and other benefits that can arise from joining a local club or other interest group. It also demonstrates a commitment to engaging audiences in the constantly changing debates about cultural diversity in this country; these are debates which do not just occur at the macro/structural levels of government policy-making, but which draw from and across all spheres of the public as well as our personal lives and interactions as individuals.

Conclusion

The idea that museums could be (or have ever been) neutral or apolitical has long gone. Extreme responses to *Identity: yours, mine, ours* and the 'Flags on cars for Australia Day' study show that museums are increasingly recognized as venues for debate and that the contestation they represent or attract can itself contribute to social and political protest and reform movements (Message 2018). This argument supports Katherine Goodnow's (2008: 148) observation that 'all representations invite dissent', and contributes to her proposition that any attempt to explore dissent, be it racist or anti-racist, requires analysis of 'the forms it takes, its timing, its sources, and its effectiveness: aspects influenced by the initial framing and the actions taken in its name'. My approach in this chapter has followed on from my broader interest in investigating dissent, which I hope can help inform improved understanding about the ways that museums can also function as an expression of resistance to macro/institutional structures and micro/everyday racisms. To do this, I have explored a range of evidence bases, including online blogs and forums which, despite not having been typically used by museum studies scholars, provide bread-and-butter datasets for discourse analysts, the value of which is articulated by Augoustinos and Every (2010: 255):

> Indeed, given the increasing salience of contentious debates in the media around issues pertaining to race, immigration and ethnicity . . . we have a wealth of publicly available data from which we can draw to analyze the finer details of how speakers orient and attend to these issues in everyday informal and formal talk.

I have also conducted a detailed archival analysis of institutional materials to consider some of the ways that changing debates, discourses, and approaches toward understanding the language and experience of racism have influenced the development (as well as consumption) of the *Identity: yours, mine, ours* exhibition at the Immigration Museum in Melbourne. Although ostensibly a book about museums and multiculturalism, I have argued in this chapter that any attempt to understand changing museum practice in Australia must consider transformations in social policy development through the same period and that this cannot happen if racism is removed from the frame. Indeed, despite its frequent marginalization from political discourse, racism (be it structural or covert/informal) exists as a constitutive form of discourse that must be recognized and grappled with publicly. I identified *Identity: yours, mine, ours* as the main case study for this chapter because of the centrality of racism to the exhibition, and because of the exemplary way that it has approached and embodied a series of conceptual and pragmatic transformations in various policy sectors and in museums themselves, which have typically had authority as a state apparatus over ways that 'difference' has been understood and accepted (or not). I have contextualized the exhibition against an overview of the way museums have responded in the last half-century to changing policy positions about multiculturalism and the public debate, which has flowed from that as part of an attempt to understand the return to racism that has played out in the public sphere and media, as well as policy sectors. *Identity: yours, mine, ours* can, in the final instance, be understood as presenting racism as a lens through which visitors can revisit the creeping issue of 'multiculturalism fatigue' to re-engage conversations about identity and belonging across lines of race, place, and perceptions of self and other. Positive, negative, and uncertain visitor responses to the exhibition provide the beginnings of this conversation in a new climate, which recognizes that while racism has returned time and time again to the national political agenda, it has never actually left the everyday experiences of many Australians.

Notes

1 Although it is beyond the scope of this book to offer a much-needed examination of the representation of refugees in Australian museums, the mid-late 1970s was critical in the formation of public opinion about them. Coinciding with public debate about multiculturalism, the Australian government made a first attempt at developing a comprehensive refugee policy in 1977, the same year in which, Neumann (2015: 13) argues, 'the arrival of "boat people" prompted unprecedented public anxieties, which, when viewed from today's perspective, appear all too familiar'.

2 For further information on the *Tampa* affair, see Chapter 2, note 3.

3 In her maiden speech to the Australian Parliament, Hanson (1996) said 'My view on issues is based on commonsense. . . . I won the seat of Oxley largely on an issue that has resulted in me being called a racist' . . . 'A truly multicultural country can never be strong or united'.

4 Kennett condemned Hanson by leading a motion in the Victorian Parliament in November 1996 to reaffirm support for non-discriminatory immigration policies and to endorse cultural diversity (*The Australian* 1996: 4).

5 This paradox is consistent with Howard's argument that:

> 'Australia's ethnic diversity is one of the enduring strengths of our nation. Yet our celebration of diversity must not be at the expense of the common values that bind us together as one people – respect for the freedom and dignity of the individual, a commitment to the rule of law, the equality of men and women and a spirit of egalitarianism that embraces tolerance, fair play, and compassion for those in need. Nor should it be at the expense of ongoing pride in what are commonly regarded as the values, traditions, and accomplishments of the old Australia. A sense of shared values is our social cement'.

> (Howard 2006a; also see Howard 2006b, 2006c)

> For discussion about the paradoxes associated with Howard's view of multiculturalism, see Tavan 2006.

6 The White Australia policy was a cluster of policies associated with the Immigration Restriction Act 1901, which limited immigration and sought to exclude all non-Europeans from Australia. The policy was dismantled in stages by successive governments after the conclusion of the Second World War, culminating in 1973.

7 Using the slogan 'For All of Us' / 'not just one of us', a central platform of John Howard's election campaign in 1996 (Gale 2001) was to appeal to the 'common-sense' of 'Aussie battlers' and sought to promise to roll-back the previous prime minister's promise of a program of national reconciliation with Indigenous Australians and support for continued funding and support for institutions of multiculturalism such as the Office of Multicultural Affairs, and the establishment of Creative Nation (Australia's first cultural policy) in 1994.

8 It is not, given this context, surprising that Drew's posters have been criticized for failing to reflect upon or challenge the assumptions and privilege upon which the 'common-sense' middle ground are based (Hashmi 2016; Frances 2016; Gupta 2017; Tan 2017). Protests by the Australian Indian Historical Society (2016) about Drew's appropriation of 'the legend' of Monga Khan, for example, do more than complain about historical inaccuracy. Their concerns highlight the issue of who Drew's posters are seeking to welcome, and by whom. Criticism that he is 'speaking for' a silent but certainly not voiceless or powerless cohort that share, by and large, the opinions that his posters promote have also been raised by Indigenous people in response to the 2017 'Real Australians Seek Welcome' campaign. Others commentators have similarly referred to Australia's colonial past when asking of the 2017 'Real Australians Seek Welcome' series: 'How does one "seek welcome" in a land that is not theirs to begin with, while simultaneously grappling with questions of what it means to be "Australian"'; particularly when politicians pay more attention to chastising 'un-Australian' behaviours and values than they do defining the term.

9 Hanson (2001).

10 Lentin and Bensaidi (2015) explain 'This dislocation of the roots of racism – colonialism, slavery, the post-immigration nation-state and its racialized borders – is ahistorical. It works to the detriment of racialized people, like migrants and asylum seekers, for whom the only "legitimate" option is integration into a framework of national identification whose goalposts are constantly shifting: the elusive "real Australian".' Indeed, in response to an incident where one of his posters had been vandalized, Drew stated that, 'unlike the previous

anti-immigration and discriminatory protests of vandals, the vandal may have been attacking aspects of "nationalism" evident in the posters, highlighting that not all Australians are heroes and instead, have committed many wrongs' (Drew quoted in Inwood 2017).

11 Hanson (2001) stated, 'I must stress at this stage that I do not consider those people from ethnic backgrounds currently living in Australia anything but first-class citizens, *provided of course that they give this country their full, undivided loyalty*' (my italics). A new language of 'core values' began to replace multiculturalism's celebration of difference and diversity throughout this period (Ang and Stratton 1998: 24; Manne 2001: 1–4; Brett 2003: 188).

12 Despite his suspicions over 'black armband history' and his general avoidance of the term multiculturalism (see Chapter 2), Howard took exception at representations of cultural difference (be they Indigenous or 'ethnic') that challenged the naturalness of white civic nationalism. This is why it is not a contradiction that the Gallery of First Australians was not criticized to the extent that the exhibition, *Horizons: The Peopling of Australia* (an exhibition that questioned what it meant to be Australian), was when the National Museum of Australia opened.

13 An event hosted by the Immigration Museum in 2017 suggested 'Systemic racism in Australia is often the result of inherited biases. If you are part of a dominant group due to your education, culture, gender or economy – these biases may be invisible to you'. *Identity: yours, mine, ours* exhibition attempts to unpack some of these issues with a process of critical thinking. The core objective of the exhibition is to make the world a safer and more inclusive place' (Ellis 2017).

14 The 'implicit assumption that "real" Australians are white Anglos' was shown by interviewees in Bailey's study in 1995: 15, and explored by high school participants in Immigration Museum (2010b).

15 One interviewee reported 'I'm very worried that the face of Australia is changing. If you mention immigration you're called a racist. I'm not, but I think it's wrong we're expected to change the way we do things to suit new people. They should change to suit US' (Bailey 1995: 2). Since opening in 2011, *Identity: yours, mine, ours* has continued to receive a minority of feedback in this vein as illustrated by this online feedback: 'They say they [the museum] are anti-racist. What they are is anti-white' (Discovery Centre to McFadzean, May 15, 2015).

16 'How can you even say anything positive about where we're at now. This racist society. Multiculturalism has failed. What are we still talking about? How can you still be talking kind of happy families at the Immigration Museum?' (Hage quoted by McFadzean 2017)

17 Internal collegial debates reflected similar concerns. For example, at one meeting a staff member: 'wondered what the pressure points for the exhibition might be and what the key contemporary issues are. He questioned what "taking a stand" meant, and wondered if the exhibition might be preaching to the converted. DTS suggested that it was the grey area at the edges of racism that was important as a focus, and hoped that the Museum could show leadership and draw a line in the sand in terms of what might be considered (or lead to) racist behavior' (Immigration Museum 2008).

18 This rhetorical shift displaces the potential impact that cultural citizenship can have (see Chapter 2).

19 The passive appeal to common-sense decency apparent in the 'I'm not a racist, but . . .' language was evident in the 1980s and 1990s, with Bailey (1995: 7)

reporting that there was a belief amongst some interviewees that multicultural-ism had caused racism.

20 A preliminary statement of intent developed for the museum said that it would 'provide a forum and catalyst for the exploration of what it means to be Austral-ian' (The Immigration Museum Consultancy Group 1994, Part 3: The Museum, pp. 3–2).

21 Di Natale (2017).

22 Australian prime ministers from 1991 to the current day: Paul Keating 1991–1996; John Howard 1996–2007; Kevin Rudd 2007–2010/2013; Julia Gillard 2010–2013; Tony Abbott 2013–2015; Malcolm Turnbull 2015-current day.

23 Associated changes extend to proposed amendments to the Racial Discrimina-tion Act (see Parliament of Australia 2017).

24 For example, 'I'm starting to get angry with some cultures', wrote a woman from Beechworth. A writer from Seaford commented that 'the decision of Jus-tice North [to return the Tampa boat people to the mainland] makes me very nervous in my own country' (quoted in Wills 2002: 74).

25 A minuted discussion about the exhibition's concept brief notes, 'MZ–IM is conscious of this exhibition taking risks. How are we talking/showing risks?' (Immigration Museum 2009c)

26 Also see Appendix 1: Academic forum facilitated by Peter Mares, November 21, 2008 and Youth Forum with the Centre of Multicultural Youth, December 5, 2008 in Immigration Museum 2009b: 15, 18). Data relevant to the develop-ment of *Identity: yours, mine, ours* is available in The Challenging Racism Pro-ject which surveyed more than 12,500 people nationwide from 2001–2008 and found that 12 per cent of Australians agree that they are personally prejudiced against other cultures, 41 per cent believe that Australia is weakened by people of different cultural origins sticking to their old ways and 84 per cent believe there is racial prejudice in Australia. About one-sixth of Australians experience racism in their everyday lives. See Dunn, Forrest, Babacan, Paradies and Ped-ersen (2011), and the Challenging Racism Project website (www.westernsyd-ney.edu.au/challengingracism).

27 There was also internal debate about the scope of the project, and the comment was made at least once that 'CM – keep in mind MV is risk averse, doesn't have a response for this' (Immigration Museum 2009d).

28 Participants in the Youth Forum commented that 'The issue of whether to use the term "race" in the exhibit was divisive', in Youth Forum with the Centre of Multicultural Youth, December 5, 2008 (p. 18) in Immigration Museum 2009b. The importance and scope of consultation is addressed at Immigration Museum 2009c: 15. The youth audience continued to be a significant focus of consul-tation throughout development of all exhibition segments, including the tram interactive. The purpose in this case was explained as being 'We wish to find out how effective this interactive will be with a specific audience – Year 9 students. It is important to capture the interest of this audience as they are often on the front lines of discrimination and prejudice either knowingly or not. We aim to make this interactive authentic and respectful of their experiences and hope to make some insights which they can carry into their everyday lives' (Immigra-tion Museum 2010b)

29 Then Leader of the Opposition, David Cameron (2007), remarked that: 'The doctrine of multiculturalism has undermined our nation's sense of cohesiveness because it emphasizes what divides us rather than what brings us together'.

30 The extent of the backlash against political correctness was nowhere more apparent than in an address delivered by Australia's conservative prime minister, John Howard, shortly after his 1996 election victory, when he stated, 'we are not a Government beholden to political correctness' (Howard 1996).

31 For example, a Hi-Lo marionette puppet (circa 1954) that has a face which has been painted with angled almond shaped eyes and a thin moustache, to give him the appearance of a Chinese man. The display uses the object to play on stereotypes.

32 Kat Clarke's hoodie 'is an expression of the different groups she belongs to – friends, peers and Wotjobaluk. She printed her hoodie with the western Victorian Wergaia language words wek (lives), wurrpa (loves) and murrun (laughs) to express her pride and pleasure in who she is' (exhibition text).

33 One of the most popular exhibition elements is a video interview with Nazeem Hussain and Aamer Rahman, stand-up comedians who have collaborated as 'Fear of a Brown Planet' since 2008. Speaking about the under-representation of diversity in the Australian media, they comment, 'I don't think Australians realize that what we export creates an image of what we are overseas. All our major cultural exports are totally white. People don't actually know really how diverse, how diverse Australia actually is' (exhibition text).

34 'Professor Fozdar said the study revealed flag-flyers were significantly less positive about Australia's ethnic diversity than "non-flag flyers" but that the attitude is not shared by all Australians. "The fact that there were significant differences doesn't mean that everybody who fly the flag feel negative towards minorities but it means that a larger proportion of them did compared with people that weren't flying flags," she said. Professor Fozdar said many people ignored her findings that the majority of both flag-flyers and non-flag flyers, interviewed by her research team, felt positive about Australia's ethnic diversity. "But that's not what gets picked up by people," she said' Weber (2012).

35 The New South Wales Administrative Decisions Tribunal upheld a complaint of racial vilification against Jones and radio station 2GB on the grounds that: 'His comments about "Lebanese males in their vast numbers" hating Australia and raping, pillaging and plundering the country, about a "national security" crisis, and about the undermining of Australian culture by "vermin" were reckless hyperbole calculated to agitate and excite his audience without providing them with much in the way of solid information'. See Administrative Decisions Tribunal NSW (2009), *Herald and Weekly Times* (2009).

36 In 2011 Bolt and the *Herald Sun* were found by the Federal Court to have contravened section 18C of the Racial Discrimination Act. They had been sued over blog posts titled 'It's so hip to be black', 'White is the New Black', and 'White Fellas in the Black' that suggested 'fair-skinned people' of diverse ancestry chose Aboriginal racial identity for the purposes of political and career clout. See Federal Court of Australia (2011); Callanan (2011); Kissane (2010); and Quinn (2011).

37 Responses at https://museumsvictoria.com.au/website/immigrationmuseum/discoverycentre/identity/. Accessed August 27, 2017.

38 A year after *Identity: yours, mine, ours opened*, the Immigration Museum had attracted 225 reviews, the majority of which do not explicitly mention the *Identity: yours, mine, ours* exhibition but present an overall impression of the museum experience (www.tripadvisor.com.au/Attraction_Review-g255100-d257176-Reviews-Immigration_Museum-Melbourne_Victoria.html [data collated October 8, 2012]).

I feel like I belong when I am made to feel welcome[1]

Studies of migration museums and exhibitions often emphasize personal and individual experiences (characteristically represented by shoes, suitcases, passports, and other personal items), as well as collective experiences (such as national or cultural traditions or events) that represent attachment to familial groups and broader imagined communities (Anderson 2006; Hutchison 2009). Migration, displacement, and belonging are represented via techniques that engage material cultures as evidence of embodied experiences of movement across places and borders. Often located on sites that are themselves historically connected to the processes and bureaucracies of migration (such as the Immigration Museum at Old Customs House in Melbourne, but also including many others like the Ellis Island National Museum of Immigration in New York, the Cité nationale de l'histoire de l'immigration in Paris, and the museum known as 19 Princelet Street in Spitalfields in London), museums also increasingly seek to reflect upon the place that government buildings and offices, and their services and officers – have in the memories of migrants, seeking in so doing to make 'audible and visible versions of the past that had been occluded or simply neglected' (Gouriévidis 2014: 1).[2] This book seeks to complement object and place-based work by exploring the infrastructure of government and institutional interactions that exist, I contend, as equivalent fields of affective experience, albeit ones that are not easily represented within museum exhibitions, either materially or conceptually. This recognition of process is important because it provides a way of understanding that rather than, strictly speaking, having made a recent comeback (see Cotter 2017, discussed in the introduction to this book), the culture wars have become a constant feature of contemporary life. Laurence Gouriévidis similarly observes:

> Ethnic and racial tensions or overt conflicts are recurrently capturing media headlines, as are the debates and legislation changes regarding the award of citizenship rights – tests and ceremonies – alongside

Figure 4.1 Model Fishing Boat – Pulau Bidong Refugee Camp, Malaysia
By Tran van Hoang, 1981. Museum Victoria HT 35674. Image courtesy of Museum Victoria.

measures passed at the national or international level to control and regulate immigration. If an *idea* of immigration is wielded as a powerful instrumental weapon in political discourse – not exclusively by right-wing groups and parties fanning a sense of panic at times of economic insecurity – migration as a *process* is a fundamental feature of the post-modern and post-colonial world.

(Gouriévidis 2014: 2)

Gouriévidis is concerned to explore the role (and production) of heritage as a 'discursive practice shaped by specific circumstances' (Littler 2005: 1) with attention to the effect of heritage on place, experiences of belonging, and conceptions of national identity. *Museums and Racism* has taken a similar approach, albeit one that emphasizes the role and practice of bureaucratic discourse (rather than place or material culture) in recognition of the often invisible – however usually taken for granted – links between museums and the political and administrative structures, cultures, histories, and doctrines within which they work. I have argued elsewhere (Chapter 3 of this volume; also see Message 2018) that it is a mistake to represent the flow of influence between government, museum, and people in a unidirectional manner, just as it is an oversimplification to represent discourse and policy at one end of a causal link and objects and exhibitions at the other. Indeed, rather than being abstract constructs, policies 'are made by women and men, and by the groups, parties and organisations they form', explains Neumann (2015: 10). I now turn to briefly explore one final example that effectively demonstrates – partly through the nature of the object itself and its interactions, and partly because of the way the object is addressed by Museum Victoria's collection data – the political and personal networks that are created by the administrative procedures and government policies regulating immigration. These networks have been invoked frequently by the Immigration Museum and sit behind many of its exhibition themes, including 'leaving', 'journeys', 'getting in', and 'identity'.

My aim in this final section is therefore to demonstrate the interconnections and relationships that exist and are generated across discursive, diplomatic, and practical fields, practices, and boundaries to indicate how the technologies, place, and circumstance of collection are implicated as much as the strategies of museum development and exhibition design in 'shaping the conduct of both the governors and the governed' (Bennett, Dibley and Harrison 2014: 140). My discussion here is, admittedly, gestural. And although I have referenced Bennett, Dibley, and Harrison's (2014) work on the processes through which 'subjects and populations come to be constituted both as objects of analysis and sites of intervention' in the nineteenth-century colonial field, my aim is to convey the importance of recognizing and representing the bureaucratic processes that are usually represented as occurring outside of the museum even today, in order to better understand how the relations of knowledge and power are composed and contested within and sometimes by museums such as the Immigration Museum.

The object I am interested in here is a model wooden fishing boat made by Vietnamese refugee Tran van Hoang in Pulau Bidong Refugee Camp in Malaysia in 1981.[3] The model boat encapsulates the role that material culture plays in signifying the experience as well as the processes associated with infrastructures of governance, at the same time as it holds those structures accountable by being a reminder 'of the courage it takes to risk the seas in search of a life free from oppression' (Zable 2015: *x*). Hoang made the model while he was waiting to be processed for entry to Australia (after being refused entry to Canada because he had tuberculosis), and later gifted it to Lachlan Kennedy, a member of the Australian Department of Immigration Indo-Chinese Refugee Taskforce. Collection notes for the object explain that the boat represents two sides of the asylum experience – the experience of refugees, and that of government officials. 'These parallel and intersecting experiences have both personal and bureaucratic elements to them. . . . The experiences of migration officials are frequently untold and unrepresented by material culture, as are material manifestations of refugee narratives' (Museums Victoria n.d.). In other words, the boat tells the story of a person – Hoang's experience of migration and the structures of migration bureaucracy – as well as the experience of interaction between Hoang and the structures of administration (represented by Kennedy, who later donated the boat to Museum Victoria).

While the small wooden fishing boat cannot be taken to represent or generalize the experience of all migrants or asylum seekers to Australia, it provides a concrete marker of a phase of immigration policy in the 1970s, in 'a country with a history that is marked by two key themes, Indigenous dispossession and immigration', and in which immigration continues to attract 'intense and vigorously contested' public debate (Zable 2015: *v*; Neumann 2015: 4; see also Chapters 2 and 3 of this book). It shows migration to be a personal and collective experience as well as depicting the mid-late 1970s and early 1980s in Australian migration history when support for refugee programs arguably enjoyed higher levels of bipartisan and public support than they do today, and in so doing, affects the humanization that Bangstad (2017) recommends (see Chapter 1).

The model boat stands out as relevant to my discussion because of its ability to draw our attention back to the processes, road-blocks, and conditionality associated with the experience of being welcomed – and not welcomed – in any new country. Not only does it exemplify the point that policy is never peopleless, it provides a material focus for the petition by writer and human rights activist, Arnold Zable (2015: *vi*)[4] for us to 'never lose sight of the individual refugee, and the tales of the countless men, women and children who have chosen to make perilous journeys, risking all on a gamble for freedom'. In so doing, the model boat can perhaps act as a reminder for us to ask the same questions regarding inclusion, exclusion, and the production of agency by museums, particularly those seeking to extend social justice aims and a 'decolonizing' agenda (see Ruffin 2017, quoted in Chapter 1). This means recognizing that the problematic trajectory and often provisional experience of 'welcome' (discussed in Chapter 3) can only be effectively conveyed by institutions committed to exploring the process of 'leaving home' (or decolonization) which requires a self-reflective analysis of the mechanisms by which power and authority are exerted *within* as well as beyond the museum.

As it has not been my aim to analyse the role of objects and collections in this book,[5] I have approached the opportunities and challenges embodied by Hoang's model boat by highlighting the interplay between museums and the structural conditions of citizenship and racism in Australia through a lens of multicultural policy since the 1970s. The book's analysis extended from this period to explore the subsequent, contingent, and shifting ideas about culture, identity, and nationalism that developed in response to the events and transformations of that era. I approached the task by profiling three episodes of institutional (and national) history related to two key case studies that effectively embody the complex interrelationships between museums, government, and public policy and show how museums engage with, reproduce, and sometimes counteract socio-political crises such as structural racism at the same time as they continue – in the case of the Immigration Museum, in comparison with the National Museum of Australia (at its opening) – to benefit from associations with government. Both the Immigration Museum and the National Museum of Australia have aimed at various times to represent a kind of disobedient museology that can critique the structural conditions that have supported their development and continuing significance in historical concepts of nationhood, citizenship, and belonging (see Chapter 1, note 5). They have done this – at least in the instances examined in this book – by bringing a focus on government policy to the forefront and seeking to represent the challenges associated with making exhibitions about policy, government, administration, and bureaucratic procedures. Moreover, rather than simply revealing social and political infrastructures for the management of difference (and hate), these examples show how museums are implicated in and impacted by everyday conditions of structural racism – by individuals against the Immigration Museum (as described in the case, for example, of the alt-right Anti-Islamic Monitor's reaction to *Identity: yours, mine, ours* in Chapter 3), and by politicians against the National Museum of Australia (as described in relation to responses by John Howard and Keith Windschuttle to that museum's opening, in Chapter 2).

This book, the second in a trilogy, has also had the task of extending the trajectory established in *The Disobedient Museum: Writing at the Edge*, which asked if museum studies has the potential to redefine a form of grounded critique that rejects the 'distance' of scholarship in favour of an intellectual activism that positions the writing about museums as a heterogeneous practice of engagement with political structures. *Museums and Racism* approached this question by examining state and national institutions that have had close associations with government policies and priorities, a selection which allows a further exploration of Bady's contention (discussed in Message 2018: 46) that critique must always be understood as a practice directed at some instituted practice, discourse, episteme, institution and that 'loses its character the moment in which it is abstracted from its operation and made to stand entirely alone as a purely generalizable' expression. As explained in Chapter 1, Star's (1999) 'ethnography of infrastructure' was particularly useful for articulating the importance of engaged and grounded research methods for museum studies, and my emphasis on internal documents, policies, correspondences, interviews, unpublished reports, and governmental 'grey literature' has sought to further demonstrate that 'grounded research' draws from different approaches and sources in different contexts, fields, and as per different research questions. In the final instance, *Museums and Racism* has sought to extend the argument made in *The Disobedient Museum* about the importance of understanding critique as a form of engaged research for writing about museums, in which the locale is often both the subject and the site of research and writing. Hoang's model boat further contributes to the importance of this argument by articulating (addressing/externalizing) and evidencing (embodying/internalizing) the complex field of encounter between an object and its context, at the same time as it invokes the discursive frames and power imbalances through which the object – and the object's maker – have come to be 'welcomed' into institutional and national cultures in Australia.

Notes

1 In 2011, the Immigration Museum distributed postcards across Melbourne inviting people to complete the sentence 'I belong when . . .' This response is attributed to Bob, Perth, 22. Online at: https://museumsvictoria.com.au/website/immigra tionmuseum/discoverycentre/identity/i-belong-postcards/index.html. Accessed October 15, 2017.
2 Gouriévidis (2014: 13) quotes Pierre Nora to explain that 'Museums as lieux de mémoire are not what is remembered, but the sites where memory is at work; not tradition itself but its laboratory'.
3 The model boat is currently on display at the Melbourne Museum.
4 Zable was a consultant scriptwriter for the Immigration Museum's opening exhibitions (see Zable 1998).
5 Objects and collections of resistance are the subject of the final book in this trilogy, *Curatorial Activism, Archiving Occupy* (Message forthcoming)

Bibliography

Abbott, Tony (2013) 'Tony Abbott's campaign launch speech: Full transcript', *Sydney Morning Herald*, August 25.

Abrams, Lynn (2014) 'Memory as both source and subject of study: The transformations of oral history' in Stefan Berger and Bill Niven (eds.) *Writing the History of Memory*, London and New York: Bloomsbury, pp. 89–109.

Abu-Lughod, Lila (1991) 'Writing against culture' in Richard G. Fox (ed.) *Recapturing Anthropology: Working in the Present*, Santa Fe, New Mexico: School of American Research Press, pp. 137–54.

Administrative Decisions Tribunal NSW (2009) Trad v Jones & anor (No. 3) [2009] NSWADT 318"], December 21. Online at: www.lawlink.nsw.gov.au/adtjudgments/2009nswadt.nsf/f1a6baff573a075dca256862002912ec/5e78e4a70e578ee4ca25768f00169e3b?OpenDocument. Accessed August 30, 2017.

Alcorn, Gay and Davies, Julie-Anne (2002) 'Jeff on the Kennett years', *Age*, October 3.

Anderson, Benedict (2006) *Imagined Communities: Reflections on the Origin and Spread of Nationalism*, London and New York: Verso.

Anderson, Margaret (2011) 'Museums, history and the creation of memory: 1970–2008' in Des Griffin and Leon Paroissien (eds.) *Understanding Museums: Australian Museums and Museology*, Canberra: The National Museum of Australia. Online at: http://nma.gov.au/research/understanding-museums/MAnderson_2011.html. Accessed September 1, 2017.

Ang, Ien (2009) 'Beyond multiculturalism: A journey to nowhere?', *Humanities Research*, vol. XV, no. 2: 17–22.

Ang, Ien, Brand, Jeffrey E., Noble, Greg and Wilding, Derek (2002) *Living Diversity: Australia's Multicultural Future, Special Broadcasting Service*, Artarmon, NSW: Special Broadcasting Services Corporation.

Ang, Ien and Stratton, Jon (1998) 'Multiculturalism in crisis: The new politics of race and national identity in Australia', *TOPIA: Canadian Journal of Cultural Studies*, vol. 1, no. 2: 22–41.

Asylum Seeker Resource Centre (2015) Elizabeth Street, Melbourne (By Peter Drew Arts), Asylum Seeker Resource Centre Facebook Page, April 21. Online at: www.facebook.com/Asylum.Seeker.Resource.Centre.ASRC/photos/a.341915052513314.75244.341910905847062/892655720772575/?type=1&theater. Accessed September 20, 2017.

Attwood, Bain (2005) *Telling the Truth about Aboriginal History*, Crows Nest, NSW: Allen and Unwin.

Augoustinos, Martha, Le Couteur, Amanda and Soyland, John (2002) 'Self-sufficient arguments in political rhetoric: Constructing reconciliation and apologizing to the stolen generations', *Discourse and Society*, vol. 13, no. 1: 105–42.

Augoustinos, Martha and Every, Danielle (2010) 'Accusations and denials of racism: Managing moral accountability in public discourse', *Discourse and Society*, vol. 21, no. 3: 251–6.

Augoustinos, Martha and Every, Danielle (2007) 'The language of "race" and prejudice: A discourse of denial, reason, and liberal-practical politics', *Journal of Language and Social Psychology*, vol. 26, no. 2: 123–41.

Australia Council for the Arts (1998) *Arts for a Multicultural Australia, 1998*, Sydney: Australia Council for the Arts.

Australia Council for the Arts (1996) *Arts for a Multicultural Australia: Policy Principles 1996–99*, Sydney: Australia Council for the Arts.

Australian (2009) 'Labor to support UN indigenous rights declaration', *Australian*, March 26.

Australian (1996) 'State backs migration', *Australian*, November 13.

Australian Citizenship Council (2000) *Australian Citizenship for a New Century: A Report by the Australian Citizenship Council*, Canberra: Australian Citizenship Council.

Australian Council on Population and Ethnic Affairs (1982) *Multiculturalism for All Australians: Our Developing Nationhood*, Canberra: Australian Government Printing Service.

Australian Ethnic Affairs Council (1977) *Australia as a Multicultural Society: Submission to the Australian Population and Immigration Council on the Green Paper Immigration Policies and Australia's Population*, Canberra: Australian Government Printing Service.

Australian Government (2017) *Multicultural Australia: United, Strong, Successful – Australia's Multicultural Statement*, Canberra: Australian Government.

Australian Government (2011) *The People of Australia – Australia's Multicultural Policy*, Canberra: Australian Government.

Australian Human Rights Commission (2012) *National Anti-Racism Strategy: Consultation Report July 2012*, Sydney: Australian Human Rights Commission.

Australian Indian Historical Society (2016) Australian Indian Historical Society Facebook Page, March 17, Online at: www.facebook.com/australianindianhistory/photos/a.993256630757273.1073741857.133280213421590/993256654090604/?type=3&theater. Accessed September 20, 2017.

Bailey, Carol (1995) *'Food's great, but . . .' Evolving Attitudes to Multicultural Australia, 1985–1995*, Melbourne: Australian Association of Social Research Conference.

Ballantine, Derek (1994) 'Station Pier seeks top ideas', *Sunday Herald Sun*, October 16.

Bangstad, Sindre (2017) 'Can there be an anthropology of hate speech?' *Anthropology News*, May 11. Online at: www.anthropology-news.org/index.php/2017/05/11/can-there-be-an-anthropology-of-hate-speech/. Accessed June 1, 2017.

Battersby, Lucy (2016) 'Aussie poster campaign hijacked by disturbing images of Rolf Harris and "Jihadi Jake"', *Age*, June 2.

Bennett, Bonita (2012) 'Encounters in the District Six Museum', *Curator: The Museum Journal*, vol. 55, no. 3: 319–25.

Bennett, Tony (2015) 'Thinking (with) museums: From exhibitionary complex to governmental assemblage' in Andrea Witcomb and Kylie Message (eds.) *Museum Theory*, Chichester, UK: John Wiley & Sons Ltd, pp. 3–20.

Bennett, Tony (2005) 'Civic laboratories: Museums, cultural objecthood and the governance of the social', *Cultural Studies*, vol. 19, no. 5: 521–47.

Bennett, Tony, Cameron, Fiona, Dias, Nelia, Dibley, Ben Dibley, Harrison, Rodney, Jacknis, Ira and McCarthy, Conal (2017) *Collecting, Ordering, Governing: Anthropology, Museums, and Liberal Government*, Durham: Duke University Press.

Berman, Gabrielle and Paradies, Yin (2008) 'Racism, disadvantage and multiculturalism: Towards effective anti-racism praxis', *Ethnic and Racial Studies*, vol. 33, no. 2: 214–32.

Blainey, Geoffrey (1993) 'Drawing up a balance sheet of our history', *Quadrant*, vol. 37, nos. 7–8: 10–15.

Bongiorno, Frank (2017) 'The statue wars', *Inside Story*, September 4. Online at: http://insidestory.org.au/the-statue-wars/. Accessed September 4, 2017.

Brett, Judith (2003) *Australian Liberals and the Moral Middle Class: From Alfred Deakin to John Howard*, Cambridge: Cambridge University Press.

Brettell, Caroline B. and Hollifield, James F. (eds.) (2000) *Migration Theory: Talking across Disciplines*, New York: Routledge.

Burke, Jason, Brace, Matthew, and Jordan, Sandra (2001) 'All Australia can offer is Guano island', *Observer*, September 2.

Burnett, Jon (2007) 'Britain's "civilizing project": Community cohesion and core values', *Policy and Politics*, vol. 35, no. 2: 353–7.

Callanan, Tim (2011) 'Angry Bolt rejects "eugenics" claim', *ABC News (Australia)*, March 30.

Cameron, David (2007) 'No one will be left behind in a Tory Britain', *Observer*, January 28.

Canberra Times (2001) Speech given by John Howard on March 11, 2001 (full transcript), *Canberra Times*, March 11.

Carroll, John, Longes, Richard, Jones, Philip and Rich, Patricia (2003) *Review of the National Museum of Australia, Its Exhibitions and Public Programs: A Report to the Council of the National Museum of Australia*, Canberra: Department of Communications, Information Technology and the Arts, Commonwealth of Australia.

Casey, Dawn (2002) 'Modern museum is meant to startle those who visit', *Canberra Times*, March 14.

Casey, Dawn (2001) 'The National Museum of Australia' in Darryl McIntyre and Kirsten Wehner (eds.), *National Museums: Negotiating Histories*, Canberra: National Museum of Australia, pp. 3–11.

Casey, Dawn (1999) 'The development of the National Museum of Australia: A museum for the 21st century', Keynote speech at Museums Australia conference, Albury, May.

Castles, Stephen, Kalantzis, Mary and Cope, Bill (1986) 'The end of multiculturalism? (The view from Wollongong)', *Ethnos*, no. 54: 4–5.

Citizenship Task Force (2006) 'Australian citizenship: Much more than a ceremony' in *Consideration of the Merits of Introducing a Formal Citizenship Test*, Department of Immigration and Multicultural Affairs Discussion Paper, September, Canberra: Commonwealth of Australia.

Civil Renewal Unit (2004) *Firm Foundations: The Government's Framework for Community Capacity Building*, London: Civil Renewal Unit, Home Office (Crown copyright).

Cobb, Amanda (2005) 'The National Museum of the American Indian as cultural sovereignty', *American Quarterly*, vol. 57, no. 2: 485–506.

Commonwealth of Australia (2008) *Australia 2020 Summit Final Report*, Canberra: Commonwealth of Australia.

Commonwealth of Australia (2002) *Select Committee for an Inquiry into a Certain Maritime Incident*, Canberra: Commonwealth of Australia.

Commonwealth Government (1975) *Museums in Australia 1975: Report of the Committee of Inquiry on Museums and National Collections*, Canberra: Australian Government Printing Service.

Cotter, Holland (2017) 'We need to move, not destroy, Confederate monuments', *New York Times*, August 20.

Council of the District of Columbia Committee on Public Safety and the Judiciary (2008) *Council of the District of Columbia Committee on Public Safety and the Judiciary Committee Report*, July 11, Washington DC: Council of the District of Columbia.

Council of the Museum of Victoria (1994) Draft Council of the Museum of Victoria Executive Meeting, Minutes of Meeting 9.00A.M. Tuesday August 30, Board Room, 222 Exhibition Street (Document marked HSS 0704.2), Strategic Management – Strategic Partnerships – Immigration Museum at Station Pier Proposal – 1994 to 1995 (SM/094/5), Museum Victoria Archives.

Cox, Emma (2014) *Theatre and Migration*, Houndsmills, Basingstoke: Palgrave Macmillan.

Cunningham Martyn Design (1998) Developed Design Report for Proposed Immigration Museum – Museum Victoria, March 31 (Document marked ASPF 1951), Exhibition Management – Exhibitions – Immigration Museum Exhibitions – Developed Design Report – March 1998, EM/042/35, Museum Victoria Archives.

Cunningham, Vinson (2017) 'The ugly, violent, cliches of white-supremacist terrorism', *New Yorker*, August 12.

Dahlgren, Peter (2006) 'Doing citizenship. The cultural origins of civic agency in the public sphere', *European Journal of Cultural Studies*, vol. 9, no. 3: 267–86.

Delanty, Gerard (2007) 'European citizenship: A critical assessment', *Citizenship Studies*, vol. 11, no. 1: 63–72.

Department of Immigration and Ethnic Affairs (1982) *National Consultations on Multiculturalism and Citizenship*, Canberra: Australian Government Printing Service.

Department of Immigration and Multicultural and Indigenous Affairs (2003) *Multicultural Australia: United in Diversity: Updating the 1999 New Agenda for Multicultural Australia: Strategic Directions for 2003–2006*, Canberra: Australian Government Printing.

Department of Prime Minister and Cabinet (1999) *A New Agenda for Multicultural Australia*, Canberra: Australian Government Printing Service.

Department of the Premier and Cabinet [Victoria] (1994) Immigration Museum – Station Pier Interim Committee Members. Strategic Management – Strategic Partnerships – Immigration Museum at Station Pier Proposal – 1994 to 1995, Museum Victoria Archives.

Devine, Miranda (2006) 'Disclosed at last, the embedded messages that adorn museum', *Sydney Morning Herald*, April 2.

Di Natale, Richard (2017) 'Multiculturalism is a wonderful thing', *GreensMPs*, March 20. Online at: https://richard-di-natale.greensmps.org.au/articles/multicul turalism-wonderful-thing. Accessed September 1, 2017.

Discovery Centre (2015) Email to Moya McFadzean, May 16, 'Enquiry number: 40758', Marketing and PR Folder, Museum Victoria Archives.

Division of Programs and Research (1997) Customs House Slide, in Presentation to the Immigration and Hellenic Archaeological Museums Committee – Public Program Development for the Immigration Museum and Hellenic Archaeological Museum, May 5, IM Exhibition Development Process 1997–98 Folder (ASPL 1991/RF1776), IMHAM, Museum Victoria Archives.

Di Stefano, Mark (2016) 'These chilling posters of a dead ISIS terrorist are popping up all over Melbourne', *BUZZFEED News*, June 2. Online at: www.buzz feed.com/markdistefano/wtf-melbourne?utm_term=.ark1pwy8E#.fixWMK8za. Accessed June 1, 2017.

Drew, Peter (2017) 'Real Australians seek welcome', *Peter Drew Arts*, Online at: www.peterdrewarts.com/real-australians-seek-welcome/. Accessed September 20, 2017.

Dunn, Kevin, Forrest, Jim, Babacan, Hurriyet, Paradies, Yin and Pedersen, Anne (2011) *Challenging Racism: The Anti-Racism Research Project National Level Findings*. Online at: www.uws.edu.au/__data/assets/pdf_file/0007/173635/NationalLevelFindingsV1.pdf. Accessed September 1, 2017.

Einfeld, Marcus (1998) 'A vision for a culturally diverse Australia: Opening of the Immigration Museum', transcript of speech delivered at Old Customs House, Flinders Street, Melbourne, November 12 (Document marked 01/03/0313), IM Professional Relations {PS} – {01} Conferences, Functions and Visits – Immigration Museum Speeches, 1998–2000 Folder (IM/PS/01/00414), Museum Victoria Archives.

Ellis, Lauren (2017) 'Racism and identity in Australia', *New Cardigan*, June 16. Online at: https://newcardigan.org/cardi-party-2017-07-racism-and-identity-with-lauren-ellis/. Accessed September 1, 2017.

Essed, Philomena (1991) *Understanding Everyday Racism*, London and New Delhi: Sage.

Evans, Chris (2008) 'Adding to the Australian family on Citizenship Day 2008', *Media Release*, September 17. Online at: www.minister.immi.gov.au/media/media-releases/2008/ce08087.htm. Accessed September 19, 2008.

Farah, Farouque (1996) 'Pieces of Greece coming our way', *Age*, August 2.

Farias, Ignacio (2011) 'The politics of urban assemblages', *City*, vol. 15, nos. 3–4: 365–74.Federal Court of Australia (2011) Eatock v Bolt [2011] FCA 1103

(September 28, 2011). Canberra: Federal Court of Australia. Online at: www. austlii.edu.au/au/cases/cth/FCA/2011/1103.html. Accessed September 1, 2017.

Fischer, Daryl, Anila, Swarupa, and Moore, Porchia (2017) 'Coming together to address systemic racism in museums', *Curator: The Museum Journal*, vol. 60, no. 1: 23–31.

Flinn, Andrew (2011) 'Archival activism: Independent and community-led archives, radical public history and the heritage professions', *InterActions: UCLA Journal of Education and Information Studies*, vol. 7, no. 2. Online at: http://escholarship. org/uc/item/9pt2490x. Accessed September 1, 2017.

Flint, David (2003) *Twilight of the Elites*, North Melbourne: Freedom Publishing.

Fozdar, Farida (2012) 'Research – Methodologies around engaging with Racism ("Flags on cars for Australia Day" study)', presentation to *Owning Racism: Can We Talk Symposium*, Melbourne: Immigration Museum, August 23.

Frances, William Scates (2016) 'New nationalist myths entrench white denial', *Eureka Street*, vol. 26, no. 9. Online at: www.eurekastreet.com.au/article. aspx?aeid=47248#.WS5WvzOB1AY. Accessed September 1, 2017.

Galbally, Frank (1978) *Review of Post-Arrival Programs and Services*, Canberra: Australian Government Printing Service.

Gale, Peter (2001) 'Representations of reconciliation: Bridges, symbols and substance' in Mary Kalantzis and Bill Cope (eds.) *Reconciliation, Multiculturalism, Identities: Difficult dialogues, Sensible Solutions*, Altona, Victoria: Common Ground Publishing, pp. 123–34.

Galligan, Brian and Roberts, Winsome (2008) 'Multiculturalism, national identity, and pluralist democracy: The Australian variant' in Geoffrey Brahm Levey (ed.) *Political Theory and Australian Multiculturalism*, New York and Oxford: Berghahn Books, pp. 209–24.

Galligan, Brian and Roberts, Winsome (2003) 'Australian multiculturalism: Its rise and demise', Paper presented to *Australian Political Studies Association Conference*, Hobart: University of Tasmania, September 29–October 1.

Gelber, Katharine (2011) *Speech Matters: Getting Free Speech Right*, St. Lucia: University of Queensland Press.

Gelber, Katharine and McNamara, Luke (2016) 'Evidencing the harms of hate speech', *Social Identities*, vol. 22, no. 3: 324–41.

Gettler, Leon (1996) 'Greek plan for customs house', *Age*, June 12, p. 9.

Gillard, Julia and Macklin, Jenny (2009) 'Australian Government to develop national statement on social inclusion', *Media Release*, July 8. Online at: www. deewr.gov.au/Ministers/Gillard/Media/Releases/Pages/Article_090709_091226. aspx. Accessed October 21, 2009.

Gillard, Julia and Wong, Penny (2007) 'An Australian social inclusion agenda', Election Pamphlet, Canberra city (authorized by T. Gartrell): Australian Labor Party.

Gillespie, Richard (2017) Interview with Andrea Witcomb, February 28, 2017, transcript, DP120100594 (Museums and Citizenship) project archive.

Gillespie, Richard (2001) 'The immigration museum' in Carolyn Rasmussen (ed.) *A Museum For the People: A History of Museum Victoria and Its Predecessors, 1854–2000*, Carlton, Victoria: Scribe Publications, pp. 363–6.

Glazer, Nathan (1997) *We Are All Multiculturalists Now*, Cambridge, MA: Harvard University Press.

Golding, Viv (2013) 'Collaborative museums: Curators, communities, collections' in Viv Golding and Wayne Modest (eds.) *Museums and Communities: Curators, Collections and Collaborations*, London: Bloomsbury, pp. 13–31.

Golding, Viv (2009) *Learning at the Museum Frontiers: Identity, Race and Power*, Surrey, UK: Ashgate.

Goodnow, Katherine (with Lohman, Jack and Marfleet, Philip) (2008) *Museums, the Media and Refugees: Stories of Crisis, Control and Compassion*, New York and Oxford: Berghahn.

Goot, Murray and Rowse, Tim (2007) *Divided Nation? Indigenous Affairs and the Imagined Public*, Carlton, Victoria: Melbourne University Publishing.

Gouriévidis, Laurence (2014) 'Representing migration in museums: History, diversity and the politics of memory' in Laurence Gouriévidis (ed.) *Museums and Migration: History, Memory, and Politics*, Abingdon, OX: Routledge, pp. 1–24.

Grant, Stan (2017) 'It is a "damaging myth" that captain Cook discovered Australia', *ABC News*, August 23.

Grassby, Albert J. (1973) *A Multi-Cultural Society for the Future*, Canberra: Australian Government Printing Service.

Gupta, Reena (2017) 'Welcome! (Kind of) The problem with being declared "Aussie"', *Overland*, March 23. Online at: https://overland.org.au/2017/03/welcome-kind-of-the-problem-with-being-declared-aussie/. Accessed June 1, 2017.

Hage, Ghassan (2006) 'The doubts down under', *Catalyst: Journal of the British Commission for Racial Equality*, vol. 3, no. 17: 8–10.

Hage, Ghassan (2003) *Against Paranoid Nationalism: Searching For Hope in a Shrinking Society*, Annandale, NSW: Pluto Press.

Hage, Ghassan (1988) *White Nation: Fantasies of White Supremacy in a Multicultural Society*, Annandale, NSW: Pluto Press.

Hanson, Pauline (2001) 'Australia, wake up!' Pauline Hanson's 1996 maiden speech to parliament, full transcript, *Sydney Morning Herald*, September 15.

Hardgrave, Gary (2003) *Twenty-Five Years of Multiculturalism: National Press Club Address by the Minister for Citizenship and Multicultural Affairs*, July 23, Canberra: Department of Immigration and Multicultural and Indigenous Affairs.

Hashmi, Zushan (2016) 'How the "Afghan Cameleer" campaign accidentally hides diversity', *newmatilda.com*, June 13. Online at: https://newmatilda.com/2016/06/13/how-the-afghan-cameleer-campaign-accidentally-hides-diversity/. Accessed June 1, 2017.

Heinrichs, Paul (1998) 'Touch-and-feel museum is true to the migrant experience', *Age*, November 14.

Heller, Nathan (2017) 'Is there any point to protesting?' *New Yorker*, August 12.

Henderson, Gerard (2003) 'Howard's odd museum choice', *Age*, January 14.

Henrich, Eureka (2012) 'Whose stories are we telling? Exhibitions of migration history in Australian museums 1984–2001', PhD thesis, University of New South Wales.

Herald and Weekly Times (2009) 'Court rules Alan Jones "racially vilified" Muslim youths', *Herald and Weekly Times*, December 22.

Hermes, Joke and Dahlgren, Peter (2006) 'Cultural studies and citizenship', *European Journal of Cultural Studies*, vol. 9, no. 3: 259–63.

Heywood, Lachlan (2006) 'National identity in spotlight', *The Courier-Mail*, November 28.

Holton, Robert (1997) 'Immigration, social cohesion and national identity', *Research Paper No. 1 1997–98*, Canberra: Australian Parliament House.

Howard, John (2006a) *A Sense of Balance: The Australian Achievement in 2006. Address to the National Press Club by the Prime Minister of Australia*, Great Hall, Parliament House, January 25. Online at: www.pm.gov.au/media/speech/2006/speech1754.cfm. Accessed September 4, 2017.

Howard, John (2006b) Doorstop interview, Hilton Hotel, Sydney, February 20. Online at: www.pm.gov.au/media/interview/2006/Interview1779.cfm. Accessed September 4, 2017.

Howard, John (2006c) Interview with Neil Mitchell, Radio 3AW (Melbourne), February 24.

Howard, John (2001) 'Transcript of the Prime Minister the Hon John Howard MP Address at the Launch of "A Stronger Tasmania Policy" – Launceston, Tasmania', *PM Transcripts, Transcripts From the Prime Ministers of Australia*, November 2. Online at: https://pmtranscripts.pmc.gov.au/release/transcript-12332. Accessed September 1, 2017.

Howard, John (1996) 'The Sir Thomas Playford Memorial Lecture', July 5, in Mark McKenna (ed.) (1997) 'Different perspectives on black armband history', Research Paper 5 1997–98, Politics and Public Administration Group. Canberra: Parliament of Australia.

Howe, Alan (2011) 'We are all in this nation's mix', *Herald Sun*, February 21.

Howie, Tamara and Roberts, Lauren (2016) '"Real Australians Say Welcome" poster display on Cavenagh Street defaced', *NT News*, May 9.

Human Rights and Equal Opportunity Commission (1997) *Bringing Them Home: Report of the National Inquiry into the Separation of Aboriginal and Torres Strait Islander Children from their Families*, Canberra: Commonwealth of Australia.

Hurst, Daniel and Medhora, Shalailah (2015) 'Malcolm Turnbull urges Australians to show "mutual respect" in battle against extremism', *Guardian*, October 9. Online at: www.theguardian.com/australia-news/2015/oct/09/malcolm-turnbull-urges-australians-to-show-mutual-respect-in-battle-against-extremism. Accessed June 1, 2017.

Hutchison, Mary (2009) 'Dimensions for a folding exhibition: Exhibiting diversity in theory and practice in the Migration Memories exhibition', *Humanities Research*, vol. XV, no. 2: 67–90.

Immigration Museum (2010a) *Personal Identity in Contemporary Australia Frontend Evaluation*, Market Research and Evaluation, March, Evaluations and Debriefs Folder, Museum Victoria Archives.

Immigration Museum (2010b) Evaluation for the Feeling Threatened Script, November 3, Tram Interactive Folder, Museum Victoria Archives.

Immigration Museum (2009a) Identity and Race in Australia (working title), Immigration Museum West Wing Gallery Development 2009–2010, Extended Project

Team Briefing, January 21, Extended Project Team Minutes, Meeting Minutes Folder, Museum Victoria Archives.

Immigration Museum (2009b) Immigration Museum West Wing Gallery Exhibition Development 2008–2010, Identity and Race in Australia (working title), Concept Overview Draft, March, Concept Briefs/Documents Folder, Concept Brief & Overview Folder, Museum Victoria Archives.

Immigration Museum (2009c) Identity and Race Project, Project Team Meeting Minutes, July 28, Core Project Team Minutes, Meeting Minutes Folder, Museum Victoria Archives.

Immigration Museum (2009d) Identity and Race Project, Project Team Meeting Minutes, August 18, Core Project Team Minutes, Meeting Minutes Folder, Museum Victoria Archives.

Immigration Museum (2009e) Notes 22/9, *Core Project Team Minutes*, Meeting Minutes Folder, Museum Victoria Archives.

Immigration Museum (2009f) Questions For Front-end Evaluation For Identity & Race Exhibition, February 24, Evaluations and Debriefs Folder, Museum Victoria Archives.

Immigration Museum (2008) West Wing Gallery Exhibition Development 2008–2010, Identity and Race in Australia (working title), Concept Overview Discussion Paper, July 28, Concept Briefs/Documents Folder, Concept Brief & Overview Folder, Museum Victoria Archives.

Immigration Museum (nd) Text in the Immigration Museum (Document Marked ASPL1971), IM Exhibition Development Process 1997–98 Folder (ASPL 1991/RF1776), IMHAM, Museum Victoria Archives.

The Immigration Museum Consultancy Group (1994) Museum of Immigration at Station Pier, October, Strategic Management – Strategic Partnerships – Immigration Museum at Station Pier Proposal – 1994 to 1995 (SM/094/5), Museum Victoria Archives.

Innes, G. (2011) ' "I'm not racist, but . . .": Zero tolerance or zero acknowledgement?', *Address to the National Press Club by the Race Discrimination Commissioner*, Canberra: Australian Human Rights Commission, August 9. Online at: www.humanrights.gov.au/news/speeches/i-m-not-racist-national-press-club-speech-2011. Accessed September 1.

Inwood, Olivia (2017) 'Multiculturalism and street art: Responses to Peter Drew's posters', *Tharunka*, March 30. Online at: http://tharunka.arc.unsw.edu.au/multiculturalism-street-art-responses-peter-drews-posters/. Accessed June 1, 2017.

Jakubowicz, Andrew (2003) 'Auditing multiculturalism: The Australian empire a generation after Galbally', Address to the Annual Conference of the Federation of Ethnic Community Councils of Australia, Melbourne, December.

Johnson, Elana (2012) 'Writing a trilogy, part two: Book two', October 15. Online at: http://elanajohnson.blogspot.com.au/2012/10/writing-trilogy-part-two-book-two.html. Accessed June 1, 2017.

Jupp, James (2008) 'A pragmatic response to a novel situation: Australian multiculturalism' in Geoffrey Brahm Levey (ed.) *Political Theory and Australian Multiculturalism*, New York and Oxford: Berghahn Books, pp. 225–41.

Kalantzis, Mary (2000) 'Multicultural citizenship' in Wayne Hudson and John Kane (eds.) *Rethinking Australian Citizenship*, Cambridge: Cambridge University Press, pp. 99–111.

Karp, Ivan, Kratz, Corinne A. Szwaja, Lynn and Ybarra-Frausto, Tomás (eds.) (2006) *Museum Frictions: Public Cultures/Global Transformations*, Durham and London: Duke University Press.

Kelly, Paul (2012) 'I'll turn back every boat, says Tony Abbott', *Australian*, January 21.

Kissane, Karen (2010) 'Case against Bolt to test racial identity, free-speech limits', *Age* September 30.

Kowtow (2012) 'Response to "Why isn't it legal to tar and feather academic wankers?"' January 24. Online at: http://falfn.com/CrusaderRabbit/?p=10847. Accessed August 30, 2017.

Lane Cove Residents for Reconciliation (2003) Lane Cove Residents for Reconciliation Submission, March 25, Submission to the *Review of the National Museum of Australia, Its Exhibitions and Public Programs: A Report to the Council of the National Museum of Australia*. Online at: www.nma.gov.au/about_us/nma_corporate_documents/exhibitions_and_public_programs_review/submissions/. Accessed September 1.

Le, Hieu Van (2011) 'Annual address on immigration and citizenship', *Department of Immigration and Citizenship Annual Report 2010–11*, Canberra: Australian Government, September 20.

Lentin, Alana (2005) 'Replacing race, historicizing "culture" in multiculturalism', *Patterns of Prejudice*, vol. 39, no. 4: 379–96.

Lentin, Alana and Bensaidi, Omar (2015) '"Real Australians" are a myth and "saying welcome" to refugees is not enough', *Guardian*, November 9. Online at: www.theguardian.com/commentisfree/2015/nov/09/real-australians-are-a-myth-and-saying-welcome-to-refugees-is-not-enough. Accessed June 1, 2017.

Light, Helen (2016) 'Beyond museums: Multicultural material heritage Archives in Australia' in Amy K. Levin (ed.) *Global Mobilities: Refugees, Exiles, and Immigrants in Museums and Archives*, London: Routledge, pp. 329–47.

Littler, Jo (2005) 'Introduction: British Heritage and the legacies of "race"' in Jo Littler and Roshi Naidoo (eds.) *The Politics of Heritage: The Legacies of 'Race'*, London: Routledge, pp. 1–19.

McCarthy, Greg (2004) 'Postmodern discontent and the National Museum of Australia', *Borderlands e-journal*, vol. 3, no. 3. Online at: www.borderlands.net.au/vol3no3_2004/mccarthy_discontent.htm. Accessed September 1.

McCubbin, Maryanne and Malgorzewicz, Anna (1994) Proposed Immigration Museum and its relationship with the Museum of Victoria. Issues for Discussion. For Meeting, Wednesday August 24, 1994, Prepared by Maryanne McCubbin and Anna Malgorzewicz (Human Studies Division), IM – Major Development Projects {MA} – {03} IM ~ MA – Correspondence and Media Clippings Regarding the Proposal to Develop the Immigration Museum at Station Pier, 1990–1994 (IM/MA/03/00180), Museum Victoria Archives.

McCubbin, Maryanne and Ladas, Nancy (1998) Australian Society Program Archival Listing, Museum of Victoria, July, Documents from Museum Victoria, DP120100594 (Museums and Citizenship) project archive.

McFadzean, Moya (2017) Interview with Andrea Witcomb, January 29, 2017, Transcript, DP120100594 (Museums and Citizenship) project archive.

McFadzean, Moya (2012) 'Exhibiting controversy at Melbourne's immigration museum', *Melbourne Historical Journal*, vol. 40: 5–19.

McFadzean, Moya (2010) 'Technically speaking: Digital representations of refugee experiences at Melbourne's Immigration Museum' in Hanne-Louise Skartveit and Katherine Goodnow (eds.) *Changes in Museum Practice: New Media, Refugees and Participation*, New York: Berghahn Books, pp. 71–84.

McFadzean, Moya (1997) Seminar Aus Studies and Michael Ames November 26, IM Exhibition Development Process 1997–98 Folder (ASPL 1991/RF1776), IMHAM, Museum Victoria Archives.

McGrath, Ann (2003) 'Diversity lost in boy's own history', *Sydney Morning Herald*, July 17.

McIntyre, Darryl (2006) 'The National Museum of Australia and public discourse: The role of public policies in the nation's cultural debates', *Museum International*, vol. 58, no. 4: 13–20.

Macintyre, Stuart and Clark, Anna (2003) *The History Wars*, Carlton, Victoria: Melbourne University Press.

Mackay, Hugh (1995, September) *The Mackay Report: Multiculturalism*, Sydney: Mackay Research.

Mackay, Hugh (1985, September) *The Mackay Report: The Multiculture*, Sydney: Mackay Research.

McShane, Ian (2006) 'Exhibitions (review of "Getting In" at the immigration museum)', *Australian Historical Studies*, vol. 37, no. 128: 123–6.

Malgorzewicz, Anna (2000) Nepean Historical Society, Transcript of Presentation Delivered at Nepean Historical Society, Sorrento, Victoria, September 1 (Document marked 01/03/0313), IM Professional Relations {PS} – {01} Conferences, Functions and Visits – Immigration Museum Speeches, 1998–2000 folder (IM/PS/01/00414), Museum Victoria Archives.

Malgorzewicz, Anna (1991) Memorandum to Andrew Reeves, January 8, IM – Major Development Projects {MA} – {03} IM ~ MA – Correspondence and Media Clippings Regarding the Proposal to Develop the Immigration Museum at Station Pier, 1990–1994 (IM/MA/03/00180), Museum Victoria Archives.

Malgorzewicz, Anna (1991) Memorandum to McCubbin, Maryanne, July 5, IM – Major Development Projects {MA} – {03} IM ~ MA – Correspondence and Media Clippings Regarding the Proposal to Develop the Immigration Museum at Station Pier, 1990–1994 (IM/MA/03/00180), Museum Victoria Archives.

Malgorzewicz, Anna (1991) Handwritten Note to McCubbin, Maryanne, July 6, IM – Major Development Projects {MA} – {03} IM ~ MA – Correspondence and Media Clippings Regarding the Proposal to Develop the Immigration Museum at Station Pier, 1990–1994 (IM/MA/03/00180), Museum Victoria Archives.

Malgorzewicz, Anna (1990) Letter to Robert Mammerella, October 10, IM – Major Development Projects {MA} – {03} IM ~ MA – Correspondence and Media Clippings Regarding the Proposal to Develop the Immigration Museum at Station Pier, 1990–1994 (IM/MA/03/00180), Museum Victoria Archives.

Manne, Robert (2001) *The Barren Years: John Howard and Australian Political Culture*, Melbourne: Text Publishing.

Manning Clark House Weekend of Ideas (2008) 'Australian citizenship: Is it really worth having?' *Weekend of Ideas*, March 29–30, Forrest, ACT: Manning Clark House.

Mansouri, Fethi, Tittensor, David and Armillei, Riccardo (2015) 'Cultural diversity through transformative action research: Translating ideas into real world impact' in *Agree to Differ*, Paris, France: UNESCO Publishing, pp. 61–4.

Markus, Andrew (2001) *Race: John Howard and the Remaking of Australia*, Crows Nest, NSW, Allen & Unwin.

Mason, Rhiannon (2012) 'Transnationalism, postnationalism, and migration', presentation to *Material Identities: Representing our National and European Selves in National Museums and Beyond*, Athens: Acropolis Museum, April 23.

Megalogenis, George (2006) 'They sank the boat, Howard says', *Australian*, February 27.

Message, Kylie (forthcoming) *Curatorial Activism: Archiving Occupy*, New York and London: Routledge.

Message, Kylie (2018) *The Disobedient Museum: Writing at the Edge*, New York and London: Routledge.

Message, Kylie (2014) *Museums and Social Activism: Engaged Protest*, New York and London: Routledge.

Message, Kylie (2009) 'New directions for civil renewal in Britain: Social capital and culture for all?' *International Journal of Cultural Studies*, vol. 12, no. 3: 257–78.

Message, Kylie (2006) *New Museums and the Making of Culture*, Oxford and New York: Berg.

Milloy, Courtland (2017) 'Surprised that nooses are being left around D.C.? Be prepared to see more', *Washington Post*, June 6.

Mitchell, Alex (1999) 'More boys in the jobs', *Sun Herald*, January 24.

Morgan, Joyce (2001) 'Howard's man: "These people are not my heroes"', *Sydney Morning Herald*, June 2.

Morphy, Howard (2006) 'Sites of persuasion: Yingapungapu at the National Museum of Australia' in Ivan Karp, Corinne A. Kratz, Lynn Szwaja and Tomás Ybarra-Frausto (eds.) *Museum Frictions: Public Cultures/global Transformations*, Durham and London: Duke University Press, pp. 469–99.

Morris, Graham (1991) Letter to Paul Clarkson, January 21, Strategic Management – Advice – Proposed Migration Museum on Station Pier – 1990 (SM/006/2), Museum Victoria Archives.

Morrison, Toni (2016) 'Making America White again', *New Yorker*, November 21.

Morton, Craddock (2008) 'The National Museum of Australia: Have we got the museum we deserve?' *ReCollections: Journal of the National Museum of Australia*, vol. 3, no. 2. Online at: http://recollections.nma.gov.au/issues/vol_3_no_2/notes_and_comments/the_national_museum_of_australia/. Accessed September 1.

Museums Australia (2000) *Museums Australia Incorporated Cultural Diversity Policy*, Canberra: Museums Australia.

Museum of Australia Interim Council (1982) *Report of the Interim Council: Plan for the Development of the Museum of Australia*, Canberra: Commonwealth of Australia.

Museums Board of Victoria (2016) *Museums Board of Victoria Annual Report 2015–16*, Melbourne: Museum Victoria.

Museum of Victoria (1997) Immigration Museum Formative Evaluation, December, Exhibition Management – Exhibitions – Immigration Museum Exhibitions – Developed Design Report – March 1998, EM/042/35, Museum Victoria Archives.

Museum of Victoria (1996) Museum of Victoria Division of Research and Collections Social History Department Collection Summary and Analysis, Museum of Victoria Division of Research and Collections Social History Department, October, MV Collection Summary Migration and Settlement 1996, Documents From Museum Victoria, DP120100594 (Museums and Citizenship) Project Archive.

Museum of Victoria (1994b) Museum of Victoria Draft Letter of Response to Immigration Museum Interim Steering Committee, Strategic Management – Strategic Partnerships – Immigration Museum at Station Pier Proposal – 1994 to 1995 (SM/094/5), Museum Victoria Archives.

Museum of Victoria (1994a) Submission to Council (Date of meeting: September 6, 1994, Agenda item: 3.2: Division: Research and Collections, Subject: Proposed Immigration Museum at Station Pier), Strategic Management – Strategic Partnerships – Immigration Museum at Station Pier Proposal – 1994 to 1995 (SM/094/5), Museum Victoria Archives.

Museum Victoria (2009) Topline Report (report No. 631T): Identity and Race – Frontend Evaluation March 28–April 1, Immigration Museum Market Research and Evaluation, Evaluations and Debriefs Folder, Museum Victoria Archives.

Museums Victoria Collections (nd) Item HT 35674, Model Fishing Boat – Pulau Bidong Refugee Camp, Malaysia, 1981, Museums Victoria Collections. Online at: https://collections.museumvictoria.com.au/items/2021625. Accessed October 15, 2017.

National Multicultural Advisory Council (1999) *Australian Multiculturalism for a New Century: Towards Inclusiveness*, Canberra: Australian Government Printing Service.

National Multicultural Advisory Council (1997) *Multicultural Australia: The Way Forward*, Canberra: Department of Immigration and Multicultural Affairs.

National Multicultural Advisory Council (1995) *Multicultural Australia – The Next Steps: Towards and Beyond 2000*, Canberra: Australian Government Publishing Service.

National Museum of Australia (2005) *Cultural Diversity Policy*, POL-C-027, Canberra: National Museum of Australia.

National Museum of Australia (1993) *Landmarks: People, Land and Political Change*, Canberra: National Museum of Australia.

Neumann, Klaus (2015) *Across the Seas: Australia's Response to Refugees: A History*, Collingwood, Victoria: Black Inc.

Nolan, David and Radywyl, Natalia (2004) 'Pluralising identity, mainstreaming identities: SBS as a technology of citizenship', *Southern Review*, vol. 37, no. 2: 40–65.

Nolan, Mark and Rubenstein, Kim (2009) 'Citizenship and identity in diverse societies', *Humanities Research*, vol. XV, no. 1: 29–44. Office of the Premier of Victoria (1993) 'Agenda 21 major civic projects', *News Release*, May 1. Office of

Multicultural Affairs (1989) *National Agenda For a Multicultural Australia . . . Sharing Our Future*, Canberra: Australian Government Printing Service.

Office of Multicultural Affairs, Department of Prime Minister and Cabinet (1992) *Access and Equity Evaluation Summary*, Canberra: Australian Government Printing Service.

Ong, Aiwa, Rosaldo, Renato et al. (1996) 'Cultural citizenship as subject-making: Immigrants negotiate racial and cultural boundaries in the United States [and comments and reply]', *Current Anthropology*, vol. 37, no. 5: 737–62.

O'Reilly, Chiara and Parish, Nina (2015) 'Telling migrant stories in museums in Australia: Does the community gallery still have a role to play?' *Museum Management and Curatorship*, vol. 30, no. 4: 296–313.

Ozdowski, Sev (2016) 'Australia's multiculturalism – success or not?' Address to the Sydney Institute, March 9. Online at: www.westernsydney.edu.au/__data/assets/pdf_file/0003/1055064/2016-03-11_Australian_Multiculturalism_-_Address_to_the_Sydney_Institute_-_Final.pdf. Accessed September 1, 2017.

Paradies, Yin (2012) 'Principles, strategies and nuances of anti-racism', presentation to *Owning Racism: Can We Talk Symposium*, Melbourne: Immigration Museum, August 23.

Parliament of Australia (2017) *Report: Freedom of Speech in Australia: Inquiry into the Operation of Part IIA of the Racial Discrimination Act 1975 (Cth) and Related Procedures under the Australian Human Rights Commission Act 1986 (Cth)*, February 28, Commonwealth of Australia. Online at: www.aph.gov.au/Parliamentary_Business/Committees/Joint/Human_Rights_inquiries/Freedom speechAustralia/Report. Accessed September 1.

Parliament of Victoria Legislative Assembly (1995) *Parliamentary Debates (Hansard 52 LA)*, Feb–Apr, vol. 422, Melbourne: Victorian Government Printer.

Parliament of Victoria Legislative Assembly (1991) *Parliamentary Debates (Hansard 51 LA)*, Mar–Apr, vol. 401, Melbourne: Victorian Government Printer.

Parliament of Victoria Legislative Assembly (1991) *Parliamentary Debates (Hansard 51 LC)*, Mar–Apr, vol. 401, Melbourne: Victorian Government Printer.

Peers, Laura, and Brown, Alison K. Brown (eds.) (2003) *Museums and Source Communities: A Routledge Reader*, London and New York: Routledge.

Penington, David (1994) Letter to Arvi Parbo, September 8, IM – Major Development Projects {MA} – {03} IM ~ MA – Correspondence and Media Clippings regarding the Proposal to Develop the Immigration Museum at Station Pier, 1990–1994 (IM/MA/03/00180), Museum Victoria Archives.

Perks, Rob (1991) 'The Ellis Island Immigration Museum, New York', *Oral History*, vol. 19, no. 1: 79–80.

Petersen, John (2010) 'Though this be madness: Heritage methods for working in culturally diverse communities', *Public History Review*, vol. 17: 34–51.

Phillips, Ruth (2003) 'Community collaboration in exhibitions: Introduction', in Laura Peers and Alison K. Brown (eds.) *Museums and Source Communities: A Routledge Reader*, London and New York: Routledge, pp. 157–70.

Politico (2017) 'Full text: Trump's comments on white supremacists, "alt-left" in Charlottesville, *Politico*, August 15.

Posner, Sarah and Neiwert, David (2016) 'How Trump took hate groups mainstream: The full story of his connection with far-right extremists', *Mother Jones*, October 14. Online at: www.motherjones.com/politics/2016/10/donald-trump-hate-groups-neo-nazi-white-supremacist-racism/. Accessed September 1, 2017.

Quinn, Karl (2011) 'Bolt loses high-profile race case', *Age*, September 28.

Refugee Council of Australia (nd) *The 'Australia Says Welcome' Campaign, Refugee Council of Australia*, Surry Hills: NSW. Online at: www.refugeecouncil.org.au/take-action/australiasayswelcome/. Accessed September 20.

Ricks, Thomas E. (2017) 'The book he wasn't supposed to write', *Atlantic*, August 22. Online at: www.theatlantic.com/entertainment/archive/2017/08/the-secret-life-of-a-book-manuscript/536982/. Accessed August 22, 2017.

Rolfe, Peter (2012) 'The legacy of Jeff Kennett's premier days lives on in Melbourne landmarks including the Bolte Bridge and Crown Casino', *Herald Sun*, October 3.

Rosaldo, Renato (1994) 'Cultural citizenship in San Jose, California', *PoLAR*, vol. 17, no. 2: 57–63.

Rosaldo, Renato (1989) *Culture and Truth: The Remaking of Social Analysis*, Boston: Beacon Press.

Rubenstein, Kim (2000) 'Citizenship and the centenary – Inclusion and exclusion in 20th century Australia', *Melbourne University Law Review*, vol. 24, no. 3: 576–608.

Rubenstein, Kim (1997) 'Citizenship and the constitutional convention debates: A mere legal inference', *Federal Law Review*, vol. 25: 296–316.

Rudd, Kevin (2008) 'Apology to Australia's Indigenous Peoples', House of Representatives, Canberra: Parliament House, February 13.

Ruffin, Ravon (2017) 'The nation we make together (Part I)'. *Brown Girls Museum Blog*. Online at: www.browngirlsmuseumblog.com/2017/07/the-nation-we-make-together-part-i/. Accessed September 22, 2017.

Samuels, Gabriel (2016) 'Posters of Rolf Harris and Isis terrorist used to mock Australia multiculturalism campaign', *Independent*, June 2. Online at: www.independent.co.uk/news/world/australasia/posters-of-rolf-harris-and-isis-bomber-appear-on-walls-in-australia-mocking-multiculturalism-a7061251.html. Accessed June 1, 2017.

Sandridge City Development Company (Sandridge) and the Major Projects Unit of the Victorian Government (MPU) (1991) Consultancy Brief to assess the feasibility of establishing a migration museum on Station Pier as part of the Bayside Development (confidential), January 21, 1991, Strategic Management – Advice – Proposed Migration Museum on Station Pier – 1990 (SM/006/2), Museum Victoria Archives.

SBS (2014) 'Hieu Van Le's journey from boat person to Governor', *SBS World News Radio*, September 2.

Schamberger, Karen, Sear, Martha and Wehner, Kirsten et al. (2008) 'Living in a material world: Object biography and transnational lives' in Desley Deacon,

Penny Russell and Angela Woollacott (eds.) *Transnational Ties: Australian Ties in the World*, Canberra: ANU E Press, pp. 275–97.

Schwartz, Larry (1994) 'Heaven's gate', *Sunday Age*, July 2.

Shoshan, Nitzan (2016) *The Management of Hate: Nation, Affect, and the Governance of Right-Wing Extremism in Germany*, Princeton, NJ: Princeton University Press.

Smith, Rohan (2017) 'Man behind Real Australians Say Welcome campaign launches most ambitious project yet', *news.com.au*, January 26. Online at: www. news.com.au/national/man-behind-real-australians-say-welcome-campaign-launches-most-ambitious-project-yet/news-story/9d8b01e793ee6211a35d183e6 a7a4603. Accessed June 1, 2017.

Soltas, Evan and Stephens-Davidowitz, Seth (2015) 'The rise of hate search', *New York Times*, December 12.

South Australian Museum (2017) #realaustraliansseekwelcome, South Australian Museum Facebook Page, January 26. Online at: www.facebook.com/southaus tralianmuseum/photos/a.478260209349.266257.66685764349/10154928656734 350/?type=3&theater. Accessed September 20.

Star, Susan Leigh (1999) 'The ethnography of infrastructure', *American Behavioral Scientist*, vol. 43, no. 3: 377–91.

Stats, Katrina (2015) 'Welcome to Australia? A reappraisal of the Fraser government's approach to refugees, 1975–83', *Australian Journal of International Affairs*, vol. 69, no. 1: 69–87.

Stevenson, Nick (2006) 'European cosmopolitan solidarity: Questions of citizenship, difference and post-materialism', *European Journal of Social Theory*, vol. 9, no. 4: 485–500.

Stone, Deborah (1998) 'A moving experience', *Age (Living Section)*, October 13.

Sunday Herald Sun (1994) 'Taking the project to the people', *Sunday Herald Sun*, September 18.

Sydney Morning Herald (2017) 'Turnbull evokes Howard on multiculturalism', *Sydney Morning Herald*, March 21.

Sydney Morning Herald (2005) 'Australia's un-doing', *Sydney Morning Herald*, March 15.

Szekeres, Viv (2011) 'Museums and multiculturalism: Too vague to understand, too important to ignore' in Des Griffin and Leon Paroissien (eds.) *Understanding Museums: Australian Museums and Museology*, Canberra: The National Museum of Australia. Online at: http://nma.gov.au/research/understanding-museums/ VSzekeres_2011.html. Accessed September 1, 2017.

Szekeres, Viv (1990) 'The role of culture-specific museums' in Donald F. McMichael (ed.) *Australian Museums: Collecting and Presenting Australia*, Proceedings of the Council of Australian Museum Associations Conference, pp. 207–11.

Szoke, Helen (2012) 'Policy – Anti-racism policy developments (Australian Human Rights Commission)', presentation to *Owning Racism: Can We Talk Symposium*, Melbourne: Immigration Museum, August 23.

Tan, Cher (2017) 'Seeking welcome while Australian', *Overland*, March 1. Online at: https://overland.org.au/2017/03/seeking-welcome-while-australian/. Accessed June 1 2017.

Tavan, Gwenda (2006) 'John Howard's multicultural paradox', paper presented to the *John Howard's Decade' Conference*, Canberra: Australian National University, March 4–6.

Tence, Maria (2009) Interview with Mara Moustafine, April 16, transcript at *Making Multicultural Australia*. Online at: www.multiculturalaustralia.edu.au/library/media/video/id/1569.Maria-Tence-on-the-Immigration-Museum. Accessed September 1, 2017.

Teo, Hsu-Ming (2006) 'These days it's harder to be different', *Herald Sun*, December 7.

Teo, Hsu-Ming (2003) 'Multiculturalism and the problem of multicultural histories: An overview of ethnic historiography' in Hsu-Ming Teo and Richard White (eds.) *Cultural History in Australia*, Sydney: UNSW Press, pp. 142–57.

Van Dijk, Teun (1993) *Elite Discourse and Racism*, London and New Delhi: Sage.

Van Dijk, Teun (1992) 'Discourse and the denial of racism', *Discourse and Society*, no. 3: 87–118.

Victorian Ethnic Affairs Commission (1995) *The Multicultural Victoria Inquiry Report*, Melbourne: Victorian Ethnic Affairs Commission.

Waldron, Jeremy (2014) *The Harm in Hate Speech*, Cambridge, MA: Harvard University Press.

Watson, Sheila (ed.) (2007) *Museums and Their Communities*, Abingdon, OX: Routledge.

Weber, David (2012) 'Aussie flag flyers more racist: Survey', *The World Today*, January 24.

Whitehead, Christopher and Bozoğlu, Gönül (2015) 'Constitutive others and the management of difference: Museum representations of Turkish identities' in Christopher Whitehead, K. Katherine Lloyd, Susannah Eckersley, and Rhiannon Mason (eds.) *Museums, Migration and Identity in Europe: Peoples, Places and Identities*, Farnham, Surrey: Ashgate Publishing, pp. 253–84.

Whitehead, Christopher, Lloyd, Katherine, Eckersley, Susannah, and Mason, Rhiannon (eds.) (2015) *Museums, Migration, and Identity in Europe: Peoples, Places, and Identities*, Farnham, Surrey: Ashgate Publishing.

Wills, Sara (2002) 'Un-stitching the lips of a migrant nation', *Australian Historical Studies*, vol. 33, no. 118: 71–89.

Windschuttle, Keith (2001) 'How not to run a museum: People's history at the postmodern museum', *Quadrant*, vol. 45, no. 9: 11–19.

Young, Marion (2000) *Inclusion and Democracy*, Oxford: Oxford University Press.

Zable, Arnold (2015) 'Foreword' in Klauss Neumann (ed.) *Across the Seas: Australia's Response to Refugees: A History*, Collingwood, Victoria: Black Inc., pp. v–x.

Zable, Arnold (1998) Fax to Richard Gillespie, June 30, IM Exhibition Development Process 1997–98 folder (ASPL 1991/RF1776), IMHAM, Museum Victoria Archives.

Zubrzycki, Jerzy (2003) 'The place of ethnic heritage collections in the National Museum of Australia', March 10. Submission to the *Review of the National Museum of Australia, Its Exhibitions and Public Programs: A Report to the Council of the National Museum of Australia*. Online at: www.nma.gov.au/about_us/nma_corpo rate_documents/exhibitions_and_public_programs_review/submissions/ Accessed September 1.

Zubrzycki, Jerzy (1995) *White Australians: Tolerance and Intolerance in Race Relations*, Canberra: National Museum of Australia.

Index

Printed in the United States
by Baker & Taylor Publisher Services